Mr. Parkinson's and Me

Mr. Parkinson's and Me

A Memoir

Simon Corpus Crispy, M.D.

authorHOUSE®

AuthorHouse™
1663 Liberty Drive
Bloomington, IN 47403
www.authorhouse.com
Phone: 1-800-839-8640

Paintings by Diego Rivera
  * Portrait of Adolfo Best Maugard 1913
  * Zapatista Landscape-The Guerillera 1915
  * Flower Day, 1925
Listed Article from David Reuben and Solomon in JAGS
Reuben, D Solomon, D: Assessment in Geriatrics, Of Caveats and Names.
J Am Geriatr Soc 37:570-572, 1989

Published by AuthorHouse   12/11/2014

ISBN: 978-1-4918-2008-7 (sc)
ISBN: 978-1-4918-2009-4 (hc)
ISBN: 978-1-4918-2010-0 (e)

Library of Congress Control Number: 2013917629

Contents

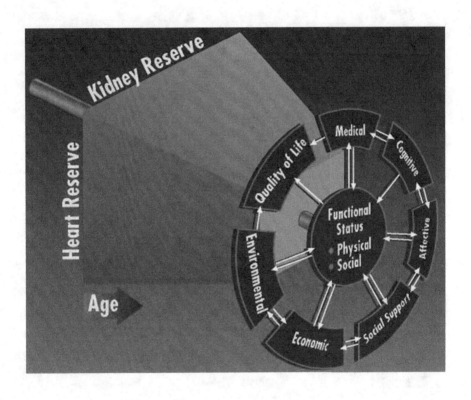

Preface

This is the story of a courageous physician. I have known him since he was a fellow in Geriatric Medicine. It is unimaginable for me to think that I could live most of my adult life with a potentially disabling neurological disease and remain as doggedly persistent in fulfilling my career and family responsibilities.

I have been a geriatrician since 1982. During that time I have cared for many individuals with Parkinson's disease. It has been, in fact, one of the more challenging and rewarding conditions I have managed in my career. During my 12 years at Emory University's Wesley Woods Center I had the opportunity to work with pioneers and experts in the treatment of Parkinson's disease. They were among the first to utilize surgical therapy, and treated thousands of sufferers, among them Mohammed Ali and Michael J. Fox. I cared for my colleagues' patients when they became medically ill, when they developed neuropsychiatric symptoms related to the disease and/or side effects of drugs used to treat it, and when they needed long-term care.

The most important thing I have learned about Parkinson's disease over the last 30 years is that the individuals who have it are less disabled, both physically and mentally, than they may appear. The slow movements and soft voice, and the resting tremor that worsens with anxiety, are hallmarks of the disease that can result in the appearance of disability. Slowness of response may be mistaken for cognitive impairment. Those with Parkinson's disease are commonly frustrated by their inability to initiate and carry out tasks as rapidly as they would like to, as well as by the stiffness or rigidity they feel at times when anti-Parkinsonian medications are not at optimal levels.

Reading this short book will give people with Parkinson's disease insights into their own condition, and inspiration to overcome the effects of the disease that may help them to remain a productive worker and responsible parent. It will also give those close to individuals as well as those who provide care for suffers of the disease a perspective that will help them understand the frustrations of living with the Parkinson's, and gain an appreciation for the daily challenges that must be confronted in order to live successfully despite the potentially disabling nature of this all too common condition.

Joseph G. Ouslander, M.D.
Professor and Senior Associate Dean for Geriatric Programs
Interim Chair, Department of Integrated Medical Sciences
Charles E. Schmidt College of Medicine
Professor (Courtesy), Christine E. Lynn College of Nursing
Florida Atlantic University

Executive Editor, Journal of the American Geriatrics Society

777 Glades Rd. Bldg. 71
Boca Raton, FL 33431-0991
Phone: 561-297-0975
jousland@fau.edu

Author's Note

In 1995, I was diagnosed with tremor-dominant idiopathic Parkinson's disease. First studied in 1817 by James Parkinson, a British physician, the disease was often referred to as the shaking palsy. Common symptoms include muscle tremors, especially in the patient's hands and feet while at rest, and muscle rigidity in the face that can make you look like you're wearing a weird Halloween mask. Balance can be impacted, accounting for the shuffling gait many of us experience. The shakes can get so bad it's tough to button a shirt or write a check to pay the light bill. Parkinson's disease seldom kills you, but it can totally disable you if treatment isn't effective. There is no cure for Parkinson's, and the disease is progressive, meaning it usually worsens over time.

More than a million people in the United States suffer from this disease. About fifty thousand new cases come up every year, usually hitting people at around age sixty and favoring, if you can call it that, more men than women, and slightly more whites than other races. Mine was a case of early onset, paying me an unwanted visit when I was just forty-two and a rising star as a geriatric physician.

While the cause of Parkinson's disease remains a mystery, medical science has figured out what's happening, or not happening, inside the patient's head. Certain nerve cells in the brain die off for some inexplicable reason. This in turn triggers a loss of the neuro-transmitter dopamine, making it tough or even impossible for the still healthy nerve cells to talk with the rest of the brain. It's like a really bad version of the cell phone ad where the guy keeps asking, "Can you hear me now?"

As more nerve cells die, the interference increases and dopamine production decreases. More calls from brain to muscles get dropped. In short, your muscles receive fewer of the correct signals from your brain that you need to coordinate muscle movements of all sorts. In fact, the scenario is even worse than that. Your brain fires off signals that actually make your muscles twitch, pulse and shake. The loss of dopamine is the main reason why signals from the brain to your muscles get totally messed up, and why your brain ultimately becomes your worst enemy. As the disease progresses, your metaphorical cell phone reception drops to almost nothing, depriving you of your ability to walk, talk, and even swallow solid foods. You can't enjoy even a modicum of happiness in life when you're in an advanced stage of the disease and when treatment is ineffective.

The good news is that because Parkinson's disease impacts muscles, exercises can prevent or reduce muscle atrophy, loss of strength, and decreased range of motion. Physical therapy can definitely help and should be part of any treatment plan. Spiritual faith, regular restorative sleep, proper diet, exercise, nutritional supplements, love and support from spouses and family, and a general overall good attitude in the face of adversity can also play a significant role in combating the disease.

The typical treatment for Parkinson's involves a whole slew of powerful drugs to control the symptoms. Most authoritative sources, including the Parkinson's Foundation, say medications are the usual first option to consider when treating properly diagnosed cases of Parkinson's disease. That's all well and good, to a point, but "properly diagnosed" is an important distinction because many cases of Parkinson's are confused with essential tremors, a condition that presents like Parkinson's to the uninitiated who don't know the difference between the two. It took almost a year before I was properly diagnosed with Parkinson's disease. The doctors I went to initially erroneously thought that I was suffering from essential tremor, or ET, as it's commonly called. The misdiagnosis meant I was taking drugs that didn't work and caused nasty side effects. My symptoms worsened. Delays in treating Parkinson's disease do great harm to the patient and should be avoided at all costs.

Considered the gold standard of drugs used to treat the symptoms of Parkinson's disease, Levadopa, also known as L-dopa, is a substance that is converted to dopamine in the brain. It's generally combined with carbidopa to reduce nausea and L-dopa's many other side effects. The drug works best in combating rigidity and slowness. It's less effective but still good at fighting Parkinson's-induced problems with balance, tremors, and coordination in walking.

Long-term use of L-dopa can cause dyskinesia, which essentially means you lose control of your muscles. You can end up involuntarily flailing your arms or legs and not be able to stop. You can lose control of your tongue, your lips, and your facial muscles. It's almost like you gave yourself a worse case of Parkinson's than you had before you started taking the drugs. Dyskinesia is a real nightmare.

Heart arrhythmia (abnormal heart rhythms), low-blood pressure, nausea, really vivid and strange dreams, confusion, extreme anxiety, rapid mood shifts, and visual and auditory hallucinations are all possible side effects when taking L-dopa even when it's combined with carbidopa. Not everyone who takes L-dopa experiences these side effects, but many of us do. The important thing to realize about Parkinson's disease is that it starts with the brain and spreads its evil touch from there. Drugs that radically impact neurological function are bound to have a variety of effects on you. L-dopa definitely does. L-dopa and other powerful drugs are about all that's available in the way of treating Parkinson's, but not quite all.

I had serious trouble with medications designed to treat the symptoms of Parkinson's disease. So, in 2002, I underwent what then was a radical procedure known as deep brain stimulation, or DBS. The U.S. Food and Drug Administration had just approved its use in the United States that very same year. Essentially, electrodes were surgically implanted in my brain and connected to a lithium ion battery implanted under my right collarbone. The electrical impulses targeted (and still do) the portions of my brain where the signals that caused the tremors came from, stopping them at the source. Deep brain stimulation has worked well for me, though with some initial horror stories I'll soon share with you, and it represents a very effective treatment for certain forms of Parkinson's disease for other patients as well.

My battle with Parkinson's began almost immediately after symptoms showed up in 1994. I struggled against misdiagnoses, side effects from powerful drugs, and incompetence in my first two surgeries for deep brain stimulation. The slog to leading a relatively normal life with Parkinson's has been long and hard. Yet, with my faith in God and with the inner fortitude one can only find in the heart and soul, I have persevered. My story, then, is one of struggle and turmoil, and ultimately it is about how I have come to live with Parkinson's, leading as normal a personal and professional life as possible.

My reason for sharing my story is to give hope to people with Parkinson's, and to give hope to people with loved ones who suffer from the disease. The disease needn't be a destroyer of life. It needn't spread suffering like a cloak of darkness over body and spirit. With love and support from spouses, family, and friends, with proper and early diagnosis under the care of a highly qualified neurologist, neurosurgeon and with a rock-solid determination to not let the disease get the best of you, there is light at the end of the proverbial tunnel. And it's not an oncoming freight train! Research on transplanting dopamine-producing stem cells into the brain continues to make progress. Stem-cell research may even result in a cure for Parkinson's someday. Until then, though, the disease remains a scourge on all of us who have it, but we have to try not to let it get us down.

I have changed the names of individuals in this story to protect their privacy. I have not mentioned most businesses or institutions by name for the same reason. The facts about the ferocious storm that hit San Antonio on Saturday, May 25, 2013, were all taken from news reports.

Here, then, is my story.

Prologue

October 9, 2002, San Antonio, Texas

The buzz of the electric shaver in my ears sounded distinctly ominous. I knew it was the setting, and what was about to happen to me that prompted my deep anxiety, bringing it closer and closer to the surface of my consciousness with every pass. I wasn't sitting in a barber shop, clippings of my brown hair clinging to one of those black plastic aprons barbers put on you to keep the hair off your clothes. I wasn't sitting in the swivel chair looking at myself in the mirror, admiring my nice haircut. I was in the hospital, and an orderly was shaving my hair off as part of the prep for my imminent brain surgery.

Even though the temperature in the hospital was cool, far cooler than the warm dry air outside in the Texas autumn sunshine, sweat moistened my underarms and ran down my back inside my white hospital gown. My blood pressure was through the roof. The nurse who had taken it a few minutes ago told me it would be a good idea to calm down, if I could. Not an easy thing to do when you know a doctor is about to peel back your scalp and drill two holes in your head, insert two mini-electrodes, and snake wires from your head, down your neck, and then connect the wires to a big lithium ion battery installed under your right collarbone.

"Almost done," the orderly said. "Then we can move you into the OR."

Then the hair was all gone. I wanted to reach up and touch the smooth skin on my head just to feel it. It's funny what we think of at times of massive stress. I resisted the urge to feel the newly exposed skin, all the while imagining what I looked like now with the places where my hair had been way whiter than the tanned skin around my forehead, cheeks, and neck. Then I imagined the sound of an electric drill with an oversize bit. The whining grew louder as the surgeon brought the drill in toward me. I imagined the bit biting into bone . . .

Don't go there! I thought. *Stay focused!*

And so I did just try to stay focused, tried to keep my blood pressure from exploding even further off the charts, tried to keep from running down the hallway and out the glass doors of the lobby in absolute panic. The orderly swabbed my skull with disinfectant to sterilize the skin. I knew my time was about to run out, that the point of no return was about on me.

Focus!

The truth was I wanted to be there. My anxiety spikes receded as I told myself that the deep brain stimulation I was paying more than seventy thousand dollars for out of my own pocket would forever change my life for the better. I reassured myself that the electrodes the neurosurgeon was going to implant would stop the tremors I'd been feeling since 1994 and that a year later were diagnosed as arising from idiopathic Parkinson's disease. Taking a deep breath, I told myself that even if I felt like the Borg, those creepy robotic beings on *Star Trek*, the operation would be worth it, as long as it worked.

The orderly was finished. "Are you ready, Dr. C?"

I said I was.

I lay down on the gurney. A nurse came in and pumped some anesthesia into my left hand through the catheter. "Relax Dr. C. Everything will be just fine," the nurse said.

The bright white lights, the sound of the squeaking wheels, the rustle of the orderly's clothes, and the controlled bedlam in the busy halls, it all gradually faded into nothing as I lost consciousness as the anesthesia took full effect.

My life would never be the same again.

1

I felt the storm stealing in from Mexico deep in my bones as I drove home after having dinner at the Outback. It was Friday, May 24, and by all appearances it was an ordinary early evening, and yet I sensed that it wasn't. Something was lingering out there, something ugly and a bit frightening. Reports from the National Weather Service office out of New Braunfels had thunderstorm warnings up, but there wasn't any hype, not really. May 2013 had been one of the wettest on record in my proud home city of San Antonio, Texas, so the stage was set for still more antics from Mother Nature. Even though the National Weather Service hadn't pressed the panic button, a pervading unease settled over me.

Thunderstorm season had barely begun and tragedy had already struck in Moore, Oklahoma, just four days earlier when a mile-wide EF-5 monster twister on the Fujita Scale had ripped a swath twenty miles long through a populated community, killing twenty-four, including children in two elementary schools. I could feel the low-pressure system sitting over San Antonio in my sinuses as well as my bones, with warm moist air cloaking my city of more than two million residents. The San Antonio River runs right through the heart of the metropolis, home of the Alamo, and Fort

Sam Houston, which is the busy headquarters of the U.S. 4th Army. In fact, a giant meander of the river practically encircles the heart of the central business district, a conglomeration of upscale stores, waterside restaurants, and other establishments. The city grew up around its fabled river, and its river sometimes lets us all know that it's still the boss.

I could see the darkening clouds on the horizon, but I paid little more than passing heed to them while pulling up to my thirty-year-old brick townhome, arriving back in a neighborhood that had definitely seen better days with my usual feeling of ambivalence. The subdivision is aged and situated near Randolph Air Force Base, one of four facilities the U.S. Air Force runs in and around San Antonio. The military is a big employer, and many air force personnel lived and still live in my development. An air force general, now deceased, once resided in my house, and late at night I swear I can hear ghostly creaks and bumps. In a way, I think it's quite fitting that the place may be haunted. I certainly am, possibly by the wayward spirit of a long-dead airman and most certainly by my own troubled past.

I guess that's one reason why my relationship with my home and my city is complicated, much like my relationship with my two ex-wives and with the elusive potential employers I've been reaching out to seemingly forever. It really doesn't pay to get sick, especially if the disease you have is difficult to diagnose and treat, like Parkinson's. It had come on slowly back in 1994 with a slight tremor and tingle in my right foot, and my life had pretty much gone downhill from there. Perhaps that's the wrong way to put it. Few lives are all downhill. There are ups as well as downs. I've always wondered about that expression, all downhill, anyway since going uphill is harder, unless you're in a Bentley.

I shut off the radio with a sigh. The big T-storms on tap for later that night bummed me out. I dislike night storms. My nights are difficult enough as I try to sleep under the plastic facemask of my CPAP. CPAP stands for "continuous positive airway pressure." A CPAP is an infernal device I must use to combat the sleep apnea that can cause me to stop breathing while I'm asleep. Unlike Parkinson's, where death is practically unheard of, you can die from a severe case of sleep apnea. People suffering from sleep apnea do not receive restorative sleep at night because the body is always under stress. You literally briefly stop breathing, which stresses the heart. In the extreme, you can stop breathing long enough for your heart to stop. Then it's all over. You wake up dead. The CPAP pumps a stream of oxygen into your lungs to prevent that from happening.

For patients suffering from Parkinson's, sleep apnea's tendency to rob you of a good night's rest can exacerbate the symptoms and increase the progression of the disease. The onset of dementia is a possibility with Parkinson's disease, particularly as you get older and other symptoms become more pronounced. I am a firm believer that lots of rest and a reduction of stress in a patient's life can slow the advance of the disease. I believe my CPAP prevents the progression of subcortical or even cortical dementia.

Still, wearing a facemask hooked up to a unit that forces air into your nose and mouth is a real hassle. If one of the hoses comes loose from the unit, you're jolted awake with a loud hissing noise. The mask has caused edema, or swelling, under my eyes that gives my face a puffy look. I was once quite handsome, or so some very beautiful women have told me, at five feet ten inches with a medium build. Now, at age sixty-one, the ravages of disease, emotional turmoil, and the simple passage of time have put excess weight on me, though at just over two hundred pounds I'm not obese. We all have our crosses to bear. As a geriatrician, I know that. As we age, the body plays tricks on us. No one is immune.

I entered the house. My cat, Tweeties, greeted me with an affectionate meow. She rubbed her nose against my leg, purring to let me know she loved me. She's a rescue cat I'd adopted. She'd been found abandoned at a truck stop and needed someone to take care of her. I was her guy. Some say cats are aloof creatures. In some ways they are, but I've always thought of them as independent and smart. I like that about them. They've been companions to me over the years as I've struggled with Parkinson's disease, fighting for employment with mixed success and disappointment as the women in my life left me like Tweetie was dumped at the truck stop, unwanted because I was no longer going to get wealthy as a doctor and because being a caregiver is something many would rather avoid. Even the potential for becoming one is enough to make some people head for the hills.

According to the American Association of Retired People, or AARP, more than thirty million Americans currently provide some sort of care for a spouse or relative over the age of fifty. With an estimated seventy-eight million baby boomers retiring and growing old in the coming decades, many more of us will provide or need care. Some will play the caregiver role, and others won't. My two ex-wives jumped right off the ship they thought was going down like the Titanic. So, I've carried on completely alone with no support from anyone, except for a brief call about once a month from my younger sister. It hasn't been easy and I'm very lonely, but I've learned that complaining does no good at all. In fact, it breeds negative energy, which is best to avoid if at all possible.

Although the sun was still up, the haze and the thickening screen of clouds obscured its brightness. Shadows filled the townhome with depressing darkness. I went around turning on lights to cheer the place up a bit. My favorite CD played on the stereo. At the moment, the staccato notes of George Bizet and the opera Carmen buoyed my spirits. Tweetie lounged in the big chair in the living room that she inhabits for much of her days, though when I go to sleep she follows me into my room to keep me company. As I proceeded with my cheering-up routine, I thought about the call or e-mail I hoped to receive from the administrator of a local clinic I'd recently applied to. I'd signed a contract of employment with the organization, and it looked promising that I'd land a better position. Of course, I'd heard that sad old story before. At the moment, I was slogging to Austin to work in an elderly care facility, and I was grateful for the work. I just wanted something better and more local, something more in keeping with my skill set.

Why haven't they called? I wondered.

I told myself to chill out, that it would be what it was, and that's it. But it's hard to psyche yourself into not worrying, and it was that way as I stalked to my stash of reiki candles. I needed to get some positive energy going. I really did. I thought about checking my e-mail yet again, but I resisted. I knew I was just making myself crazy.

I often take solace in my religion, finding peace through my faith as a Christian. I also take solace in reiki, in spite of the fact that I am and always have been a devout Episcopalian. Yet, I know there is more in the spiritual realm than organized churches. I've come to cherish both the religious and the spiritual arenas of the mind and soul, and, really, aren't they both bound together in ways that defy our ability to truly fathom what is and isn't real?

Reiki is a combination of two Japanese words that describe a spiritual, nonphysical alternative medicine focused on positive life energy that heals. It is believed that health derives from the Ki, which flows through you and animates the body's organs and tissues. An interruption or interference with the Ki will cause illness, which has made me think more than twice that my Ki got snarled in traffic on a freeway in Los Angeles. Reiki candles, made from wonderfully aromatic blends of different oils, are thought to encourage the Ki, giving it the wide-open road in Kansas or in big-sky New Mexico. You can focus the positive energy on yourself, your pet, or pretty much anything. No matter what I'm focusing on, I find the scent of my reiki candles calming and relaxing.

I lit my favorite reiki and focused the Ki on me, as opposed to Tweetie, the ghost of the dead general living with me, and the grand city of San Antonio. I needed to be selfish with my Ki. Sometimes you just have to take care of yourself. Heaven knows. You can't really count on anyone else when it all comes down to brass tacks. I picked Tweetie up, and sat down with her in my lap, luxuriating in her company. I let the genius of Ravel and Pavane une Infante De' Fante soothe me. I had the feeling that it was going to be a very long night.

2

The good meal and the excellent music combined with the aroma of the reiki candle to ease my anxiety. I suppose I was more nervous about the results of my job interviews at the clinic than about any approaching line of thunderstorms. It was logical to think so. I'd been battling job discrimination for years, and frankly I was simply worn out. With no one to talk to about it, with no one to hug and hold tight, with no one who really loved me for who I was now, my foul mood did not rise to the altogether unusual. But breathing in the scent of the candle was a welcome comfort. The warmth of my precious kitty in my lap was too.

I let my mind wander back in time to days when the world seemed limitless in its possibilities, back to when all I had to worry about was what I'd do after school as a somewhat introverted and nerdy kid growing up in San Antonio. The city was much quieter in the late 1950s, almost sleepy. I guess the entire world was that way when compared to the frenetic present, with the exception of the duck-and-cover panic of the Cold War that has given way to the shit-in-your-pants fear of terrorism. We had Elvis and we briefly had Edsels. We had *Rock Around the Clock* from Bill Haley and the Comets the same year Ford introduced its flop new car.

We had poodle skirts and *I Love Lucy*. We don't have any of the old anymore, and maybe that's just as well. As I sat thinking about my life, it struck me that nothing is as constant in this world as unstoppable change with the inevitable passage of time.

My dad, who died in August 2012, was born in Alsace, France, and when I was growing up some of my friends from school thought having a French father was super exotic. He earned a living as a general practitioner and surgeon, which meant my mom, my sister, and I led a solid upper-middle class existence in a nice suburban neighborhood. I collected stamps and coins with a passion, and I loved model trains and slot-car racing. In high school at the Texas Military Institute, I became more athletic, racing bicycles and playing varsity tennis. My dad loved sports cars, and one day he took me out for a speedy spin in his 911 Porsche. The ride remains with me even now. It stands out as a moment when my father and I felt truly close, which wasn't the case as I grew older and defied his wishes that I follow in his footsteps to become a general surgeon like him. There seems always to be a nexus of conflict built into the relationship between boys and their dads, and it was no different with us.

If I had to describe my childhood and teen years, I'd use the words serene and idyllic. My mother was always distant, detached, and oddly prone to wild mood swings, and I'm convinced now that she was bipolar. Yet, her condition didn't impinge on our lives in any significant way. Later in her life, my mom developed Parkinson's disease, predisposing me to it. Some think you can be more likely to get the disease if it's in your family. That's common with other diseases as well, such as breast cancer. Eventually, she couldn't walk and had to get skilled nursing care.

Treatments for Parkinson's disease have progressed since she was diagnosed. Now some treatments can slow the advancement process, but she didn't get the benefit of what's available now. She died after being dropped at the care facility where she was living, severely fracturing her femur. She bled to death as a result. I've always thought her death must have been horrifying, and I try not to dwell on it too much.

My past may indeed haunt me, but it's not the past of my upbringing. It's the past of my later years. My earlier memories sustain me these days, at least to a certain extent. I remember dates with my high school girlfriend in my dad's 454 Cutlass 442, and sneaking with my girlfriend onto a neighbor's lawn to make passionate love under the moon and stars on a sultry late spring night after graduating from the Texas Military Institute. I treasure recollections of my innocence and hers. I sometimes wish I had both back.

My undergraduate years as a Sociology Major at Trinity University in San Antonio were when the seed of becoming a physician really took root. As I've said, my dad was pushing for me to become a general practitioner and surgeon, and I bought into it. A son wants to please his father. There's no shame in it. The problem is that the son isn't the father, and so blindly following like a sheep, or a lemming, is often a very bad idea.

In 1973, he set me up to work a summer internship as a surgical assistant where pre-med students were allowed to assist top surgeons. I can still recall what it was like to put my fingers around a patient's ruptured aortic aneurysm while working with a renowned cardiovascular surgeon, and I can still recall what it was like to turn the leg of a patient undergoing a hip replacement. Such moments become indelible on the mind of a young and ambitious man anxious to please his father and himself. Ego runs wild. The world seems to be the proverbial oyster.

If a dream is born of a falsehood, it is bound to fizzle out. Such was the case with my tenacious desire to follow in my dad's footsteps. The beginnings of my revolutionary pursuit of my own individuality began at about the same time. I became fascinated with sociology and anthropology, and I went for a dual major in each subject. The study of people that leads to an intimate understanding of the physical and psychological side of humanity is at the very heart of gerontology, and it was at Trinity University that my ultimate destiny was forged. Still, heeding my father's influence, I pursued a path that was untrue to myself. For three years I struggled with pre-med classes that were supposed to lead me to graduate school and a livelihood as a prosperous surgeon, and for three years I floundered.

"If you don't get accepted into medical school in the United States, you might as well become a shoe salesman," my dad said during a heated discussion about my career path. "You can't take any shortcuts."

"But Dad," I said, "I'm not sure this is what I want to do."

"People do jobs they don't like all the time. Being a surgeon is an honor and a privilege. It's something you have to want with all your heart. Do you want to sell shoes?"

I told him that I didn't like the idea of selling shoes. Frankly, messing with people's feet all day grossed me out. It was like putting on rented shoes from a bowling alley—not very appealing. The courses I was taking, though, focused largely on memorizing various aspects of calculus, chemistry, and physics. The preliminary training I was receiving did not dwell much on medical and clinical science, both of which are essential in preparing a person to become a medical doctor. Ultimately, I did not get into an American medical school. Instead, I ended up studying medicine at the Universidad Autonoma de Nuevo Leon(UANL) in Monterrey, NL, Mexico. According to my dad, the shoe fit.

Although San Antonio is only one hundred and fifty miles from the Mexican border and did and does have a strong Hispanic presence in terms of culture and population, I wasn't steeped in the ways and the language of my neighbors to the south. Indeed, the transition from Texas to Mexico added to the stress I was already feeling. Looking back on things now, I can see that the foundation for my early onset of Parkinson's disease was laid in my twenties. My mother's affliction with Parkinson's quite possibly predisposed me to the same illness, and stressors, both internal and external, contributed to its development in my brain as well. At the time, of course, I knew nothing about my future and possibly wouldn't have cared if I had. Youth is like that, sad to say.

I struggled mightily to master the language and my courses during my first semester. I flunked gross anatomy and histology. My dad called me and voiced his concern that I was literally pissing my life away down in Mexico. I started to have nightmares about patent-leather loafers. I worked like a demon. Gradually, I became fluent in Spanish and began excelling in my courses, in spite of the insufferable heat. Often, the temperature exceeded 110 degrees Fahrenheit. Before I finished medical school in 1983, I fell for a beautiful American coed. We loved each other in the youthful way that kids love. The relationship disintegrated after she demanded marriage and I expressed qualms. In retrospect, the breakup was for the best, but it marked the first of my many failures with women—disasters in part of my own making and in part due to my tendency to gravitate toward ladies that seem always to end up badly hurting me.

Bright incandescent lights outside my townhome banished the complete darkness of the night. I stood on my upper patio staring at the same sights I'd seen for years, ever since I'd foolishly sold some prime San Antonio real estate to buy this dump so my second ex-wife could live closer to her family. It's absolutely astounding what a man will do for love and companionship, and especially sex, and I'm certainly no exception. I can be as dumb as the next guy. There's no doubt about that. The only good thing to come out of my second marriage was my son, who is now seven years old.

Strangely enough, we were both born on the twenty-first of June. We are both children of the summer solstice. I think about that sometimes, about how out of all the other 364 days of a calendar year my son's birthday happened to coincide with mine. Is there really such a thing as a coincidence in life, or is everything written in a celestial book of some kind and we really have no free will over our destinies? Such a thought is terribly depressing.

Even if we screw up our lives, I'd like to think we had a hand in it and that it was not predetermined before we were even born. I'd like to think that God didn't fate me to Mr. Parkinson's as a constant and unwanted partner since my early forties. It is a question humans have asked through the ages: How could a loving God predetermine or sanction diseases, pandemics, world wars, genocide, natural disasters, famine, pestilence, cruelty and all the rest of life's horrors that are visited upon billions of people on this planet? How could all this be the will of God? How could my disease be God's will? How could anybody's disease be so? I don't have the answers. I guess nobody does, except possibly God, and he's not talking.

Looking out at the other units, I breathed in the humid air and gazed skyward. Not a star shone through the thickening cloud cover. I hadn't expected to see any sign of the heavens, but I stared up anyway with my time as a medical student in Mexico weighing heavily on my mind. Thirty years ago almost to the day was when I graduated from the University of Nuevo Leon Faculty of Medicine as a medical doctor. It was a proud moment for me, though I think my dad considered my education second-rate, which diminished in his mind the breadth of my hard-won accomplishment. My medical school days seemed like another life, and the period of my existence really was different. So much had changed for the good and the bad. So much life had rushed by like that proverbial river we all talk about, but don't appreciate until we're facing the twilight of our own short day as living sentient beings.

I thought about all the elderly patients I'd seen in those intervening decades. Getting old can be a difficult and painful experience, especially when a long-loved spouse dies or you suffer from health problems that plague every waking moment. I become a geriatrician not so much for the money. I chose this field of medicine because I felt compassion for people entering their final stages of life, and because I thought I could help make the passage more bearable for them. I pictured all their faces— craggy, wrinkled, liver-spotted, sagging, and yet grand in a way that bespoke the wisdom that can only come from living long. I pictured myself with my extra weight, the swelling under my eyes, and the place under my right collarbone that contained and still contains a lithium ion battery that constantly shoots electrical impulses deep into my brain.

How strange life is, I thought. *How very strange.*

A brilliant flash of lightning illuminated the far horizon. In the distance, I heard the low rumble of thunder above the swish of passing cars on the adjacent road.

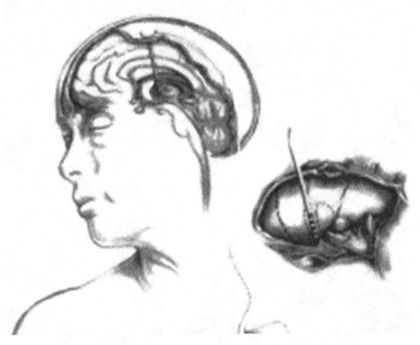

DBS illustration (c) Medtronic Corporation. 2013

3

Green, yellow, and red blobs from Doppler radar returns pulsed on my TV like some hideous post-modern art painting, but I wasn't looking at the output from a talented or not so talented artist. I was watching The Weather Channel and not liking what I saw. High-pitched beeps alerted me to the crawl on the bottom of the screen, warning of violent approaching T-storms that had rapidly gained unexpected strength. The pretty blonde anchorwoman stood with her back to the map and somehow still knew where to point without looking. She said a strong line of thunderstorms had formed about three hundred miles to the west of San Antonio in the northern mountains of Mexico and around Big Bend as a result of an upper-level disturbance on Thursday. Then the storm front had slowly migrated eastward, pushing an outflow boundary, or a wall of dense rain-cooled air containing high winds. The outflow boundary, or gust wall, was about to collide with the low-pressure system sitting above my head. It was a meteorological bomb slated to train from south to north right over the city.

This can't be good, I thought, as I stroked Tweetie's head and yawned.

It was getting late. The day had been long and sadly uneventful from an employment perspective. At least dinner at the Outback had been good, as usual. I read the crawl again as it looped across the bottom of the screen for the umpteenth time. White letters on a red background.

Beep! Beep! Beep!

The sound cut out on the anchorwoman and the mechanical voice of the National Weather Service audio robot echoed through the speakers of my TV. "Severe thunderstorm warning for San Antonio. Winds in excess of sixty miles per hour and golf-ball-size hail could occur in the warning areas. Rainfall in excess of two inches or more per hour. Flash floods in low-lying areas . . ."

"Been there, done that," I muttered. "Bought the wet T-shirt."

I put Tweetie down and shut off the TV. I hesitated for a long moment. The anxiety I had felt earlier had diminished somewhat while I listened to Ravel Daphne et Chloe': Suite No.2 and basked in the scent of the reiki candle, but the unease had now returned in force. Resigning myself to the fact that the night was bound to become boisterous, I padded off to my bedroom to get some shuteye before the shit really hit the fan. At my bedside was the hated CPAP with its clear plastic mask and accordion gray plastic umbilical hose. I fitted the mask over my face, tightened the harness that kept the mask in place, and then turned the machine on.

Hiss . . .

Once I was sure the mask was properly seated and that the CPAP wasn't going to wake me up, I turned off the light and settled down to sleep. I smiled slightly beneath my mask, thinking that it was ironic that I should be worried about a little hiss from a breathing machine when all hell was about to break loose outside. I couldn't fall asleep right away, but after awhile I must have dozed off because I jolted awake out of a quasi-sleep. Lightning in triple troika moving horizontally illuminated the window.

"One Mississippi . . . two Mississippi . . . three Mississippi . . . four Mississippi. Oh, hell," I grumbled. "It's still miles away."

Boom!

I closed my eyes, and for some strange reason I couldn't discern I pictured my first ex-wife, Wendy, a thin and curvy blonde with shining blue eyes and a laugh that still enchants me when I replay it in my mind. Perhaps I summoned her at that moment in my drowsy state because I felt lonely and wanted to relive a happy period of my life as a young man. I remembered meeting her in the cafeteria at the hospital where I was doing a residency in family medicine in Ohio. It was in the late 1980s. We were young and full of hope and steeped in the innocence that only time and mistrust can erode. I sat across from her and smiled, immediately smitten. I looked at the strange white-dough thing on her plate and asked her what it was.

"It's a pirogue," she said with a laugh. She took a bite. "You don't know what a pirogue is?"

I was temporarily speechless. The effect she had on me was nothing short of nuclear. "I, uh, well . . . no. You see, I'm from San Antonio. They're more Tex-Mex down there. They don't make p—"

"Peer-o-gees," she said. "They're delicious. It's basically dough with a luscious filling of potato or sausage or cheese or whatever."

"Oh," I said. "Sounds, uh, good!"

"Try one!" she said, and plunked a pirogue down on my plate.

I tried the pirogue. It was out of this world. I couldn't take my eyes of her as we introduced ourselves. After that day, we began to spend as much time together as we could. Unfortunately, it wasn't all that much because of our circumstances. She was still in school working toward her bachelor's degree in psychology. I was slaving away as a resident, the low man on the totem pole, and putting in so many hours that sleep was a veritable luxury I grew to crave more than food or drink or sex. Every doctor goes through this, but that doesn't make the process any less brutal. When I finished my residency in 1990, I was offered a two-year fellowship in geriatric medicine at a prestigious university in California. For me, the opportunity was a godsend, an indication that my choice of career paths was a good one. I felt a fair degree of vindication from the standpoint of my dad's often voiced doubts. I felt like I was on my way, and Wendy was agreeable to sharing my life. I wanted to share hers too.

All of these memories rushed back in bold relief as I lay in bed listening to the rumble of distant thunder over the wretched CPAP. A sense of deep regret filled me when I pictured Wendy and I at Lake Chautauqua in upstate New York, sitting on a dock dangling our bare feet in the chilly water and watching a mother duck with her ducklings swim nearby. We held hands and talked about the new horizons that awaited us both. The hope and innocence of youth filled our hearts with anticipation about our future prospects.

"It's so beautiful here," Wendy said, giving my hand a squeeze. "Just look at those cute ducklings!"

I smiled and squeezed her hand back. My feet were getting cold in the water, but I didn't want to leave the dock. I didn't want to break the moment. "I love how they follow mother duck in a line like that," I said.

Wendy laughed. "You won't get kids to do that," she said, shaking her head.

I nodded in agreement. I couldn't help but think of the reticence Wendy had always shown when the subject of kids came up. She didn't appear to relish the idea of being a mother, unlike the duck we were both watching intently. The subject of our having kids didn't come up often as a consequence. It was a shadow lurking in the background of an otherwise apparently idyllic relationship.

As we sat on the dock, we could hear music in the background. Tents had been set up for a music festival on the lakefront. It was a full-blown affair with bands, food vendors, and amusement rides for kids. It was a family event, and I'd been fleetingly aware of how that made me feel. I suppose I had romantic notions of marriage and having a family of my own, though to this day I am still not sure if it was romance or not. Perhaps it was my desire to conform and be like everyone else. All I remember is feeling a powerful love for Wendy, one I thought would never end. The world seemed wide open. The brightness of our future burned like the rising sun.

We were married soon after that, and then we moved to California where we rented a cheap apartment and got down to work.

Those days in California were among the happiest of my life, and looking back on them now I wonder at the amazing twists and turns that go into a person's existence on this earth. I wonder at how things can go so happily right and suddenly make a one-hundred-eighty-degree turn and go in the opposite direction. The fellowship was very demanding, sending me to train at various centers operated by the Veteran's Administration, homes for the elderly, geriatric evaluation and management units, and so on. It was also publish or perish. Research papers and chapters for books on gerontology crowded my days and nights, and Wendy began to feel ignored and unappreciated. Yet, there were times of great joy and a feeling that we were on our way to a better life together, so we tried not to let the pressures that any budding physician faces do harm to the love we shared.

One of my fondest times on a professional basis was when I served as a part-time medical director in a facility operated by the motion picture and television guilds. Elderly actors, screenwriters, grips, gaffers, costume makers, seamstresses, virtually any and all who had been involved in some way with film, were given care at a very low cost in a wonderful setting that even featured putting greens. On movie nights, famous directors would act as docents and regale the aged audience with stories about the films we were about to watch, films that the director-docents usually had made long ago. The past was very much in evidence everywhere in the facility, with sepia autographed black-and-white pictures of glamorous actors and actresses adorning the walls. The cinema and photography have always been a passion of mine, and I think much of that passion stirred to life while I was blessed with the company of the creative people I was helping at the guild facility.

When my fellowship ended, Wendy and I moved back to San Antonio, where I took a job at a health maintenance organization working with geriatric patients. Many were poor and in dire condition. The HMO did not appear able to deal with the patients. It was just my bad luck to have happened on a facility that was right out of any nightmare medical scenario with patients lying unattended in their beds, with a shortage of doctors, and with administrators that behaved like freaked out ostriches, burying their heads in the sand and hoping everything would turn out for the best. I saw almost immediately that the job wasn't right for me, and I started looking around for something else. It was good that I did because the HMO closed down.

Wendy and I ended up back in California in 1994. I was working as the chief of geriatric medicine at a teaching hospital and putting in long hours, as usual. I was also on my way to a tenure-track professorship at the university. I would be teaching gerontology and practicing it as well. It seemed ideal. Then, in the fall of 1994, I became aware of a strange sensation in my right foot, especially at night while I was trying to fall asleep. I ignored it at first, but the sensation did not go away. The medical term for it is "fasciculation." As a physician, I knew it was foolish to ignore symptoms like that for long, and so I soon made an appointment with my internist.

"You're just anxious, Dr. C," the internist said. "I don't see that there's anything wrong with you at all."

"Well, I think there is," I said. "It feels like there's a bug crawling on my toes. It's driving me crazy!"

"Doctor, heal thyself. Is that it?"

"No, that's not it. I'm having a problem here," I said. "I need your help to find out what it is."

The internist ordered some tests and prescribed anti-anxiety meds. The tests turned up nothing and the meds made it hard to carry out my duties. I felt exhausted all the time. Then I began to notice a difference in the way I walked. Although it was only slight at first, I couldn't seem to easily put one foot in front of the other like I had for all my life. I could still walk okay. It just wasn't a completely normal walk. It took a little more effort. I was worried. The slight quivering in my foot worsened until I had an actual intermittent tremor that I couldn't control. I went for more tests, but the doctors didn't have a clue about what was wrong with me. My frustration and depression intensified, and I guess people at work noticed. One day, the chairman of the faculty called me into his office.

"Dr. C, I've been getting complaints about your work performance."

The man looked like an aging woodchuck with shocks of thin white hair. His voice was high-pitched and profoundly irritating, and his eyes were devoid of any compassion whatsoever. I knew he wasn't receiving complaints about me, but I also knew he was well aware that I'd had to take more time off than I should have to go to doctor appointments. My gait was starting to suffer at that point, and the chairman clearly didn't like it. Perhaps he thought I was drunk.

"Show the complaints to me," I said.

"I don't have to do that, and I won't," Dr. Rodent said.

"Yes, you do! I have a right to see any formal complaints against me."

"I want you to see a behavioral counselor. I want you to work on your attitude."

The man was raising his voice. My temper flared. We exchanged words. I told him I didn't need a behavioral counselor. He'd been harassing me for no apparent reason, except that I was struggling with symptoms nobody could pin a cause on. My wife had grown increasingly distant as well. Within a matter of months, everything I'd worked to build during the course of my adult life seemed ready to topple over into a pile of debris.

"I think it would be best if you resigned your position," Dr. Rodent said. "You don't seem able to handle your job responsibilities. You've fallen behind in your work."

I saw the writing on the wall. I knew he would continue to relentlessly harass me. When a boss decides you're out, you're out. At that point, I was beyond tired. I'd sunk into deep depression. It just didn't seem worth it to fight.

What is wrong with me? I asked myself repeatedly, until it became a tragic mantra.

"I will resign," I said, noting the immediate look of relief that crossed the odious man's face. He almost smiled. "I will resign as long as the letter says I left in good standing."

Dr. Rodent smugly agreed.

I left his office feeling as though I'd been mugged, and in a way I had been. I left the building and got into my car. My hands shook from anger, or at least I hoped that was what made them shake. My damned right foot shook too. My breath was short. It was hard to breathe. My heart beat fast and I knew my blood pressure was skyrocketing. I willed myself to calm down, but it wasn't easy. The snarled traffic on the freeway didn't help soothe my shattered nerves as the shock of it all hit me hard. I was suddenly out of a job and facing a worsening illness no physician had yet properly diagnosed.

4

Christmas Eve of 1994 in San Antonio rang in with me sitting in a little apartment alone with the cats. I savored a cigar with a glass of fine cognac. I'm not usually a smoker or drinker, but on special occasions I indulge. Spending Christmas Eve by myself wasn't special, of course, but I figured I should make the best of it. What else could I do? When life gives you lemons, you make lemonade, if you can. Wendy had decided to go visit her parents for the holidays, and she'd made it abundantly clear that I wasn't invited or even wanted.

"I just need time to think, Simon," she'd said a few days earlier. She ran her right hand through her beautiful golden hair and fixed me with the same stare she gave the cats when they clawed at the sofa instead of their scratch pads. "You understand, right? It's been very stressful around here lately. I need a break. You need a break. *We* need a break."

"I don't understand. We should be together. It's going to be Christmas time, for heaven's sake! I don't want a break! I need you here! With me!"

She kept her voice low and stern. "I think it'll do us both a world of good if we give each other some space right now."

The conversation devolved into a fight. We'd been fighting a lot lately, especially after I'd been forced to resign and return to San Antonio. I'd lined up a new job at a family care clinic, but that wasn't the point. Wendy had envisioned a husband who was an important man on campus, a fellow to be reckoned with, a gent with big bucks, a big house, and a bigger bank account. A Lexus or a Beamer wouldn't have hurt either. She'd nearly come right out and said as much when I arrived home and told her what happened with Dr. Rodent. She stalked out of the living room and closed the bedroom door. She didn't come out for a long time. She didn't even say she was sorry I'd had to quit. It was then that I began to seriously wonder about our marriage.

I took another drag on the cigar, inhaling just a little of the smoke. The alcohol warmed me from the inside out and drove the loneliness and anger I felt off a short distance. It was like a pack of wolves hovering just outside the perimeter of light from a campfire. As I smoked, I noticed that the tremor, now full-blown whenever the foot was at rest, decreased slightly. The discovery piqued my curiosity. I asked myself if there could be a correlation between the smoke and the reduced shaking. At the time, I wasn't sure. My body was playing cruel and persistent tricks on me, leaving me at a loss as to what was happening. The not knowing was almost as bad, or maybe even worse, than the actual physical symptoms that were starting to manifest in more aggressive ways. I went to bed early on that night before Christmas. I remember lying in bed and staring up at the ceiling in the dark. I wondered what Wendy was doing at that very moment. No doubt she was laughing and sipping eggnog with her family. Christmas music would be playing in the background. The house would smell of the ham dinner they'd eaten earlier. The tree would sparkle with tinsel and blinking colored lights. The desolation that swept over me then caused me to turn over and hide my face in the soft pillowcase, which soon was wet with my tears.

The peel of thunder shook my townhome and jolted me awake as if someone had fired a pistol in my ear. I literally gasped. Having been in a deep REM sleep just seconds earlier I was slightly disoriented. The lightning outside lit up the darkened room in a brilliant white light. I groaned, turned off the CPAP, and checked the clock on the night table beside the bed. It was nearly three o'clock in the morning. Torrents of rain pounded on the roof and windows. I heard the rush of the water in the gutters. I could tell by the sound they made that the rain was overflowing in them and cascading down to the pavement below. Wind lashed the building with fierce gusts.

I got up, thankful that the power hadn't cut out, and switched on the lights. The power will sometimes fail in San Antonio when a real corker of a T-storm rips through, blowing like a freight train across the beautiful hill country in south-central Texas. It's big country out here, and we've got the storms to go along with it. On this night, the thunder gods were pulling out all the stops. Now totally awake, I looked for Tweetie and saw her casually sitting there, her head cocked to one side. Her tail whisked back and forth. She seemed almost amused at my momentary befuddlement.

"Come on, Tweetie," I said as I stooped to pick her up. She felt warm and soft in my arms. She felt comforting in the raging storm. I padded to the office and turned on the lights. What I saw horrified me. Rainwater had leaked from my upper patio onto my gorgeous and very expensive leather-top desk and destroyed the keyboard of my desktop computer. Frantic, I put Tweetie down and mopped up the mess, thankful that I'd gotten to it in time. By waking me up when it did, that peel of thunder had spared my desk, a piece of furniture I loved and that represented the promise of lost happier times in the past. I quickly placed big black plastic garbage bags over the desk to protect it, and I moved the desktop out of the way. I tried to see where the leak was coming from, but I couldn't. I got some pans from the kitchen and put them on the desk, hoping to catch the water dripping down.

With my desktop out of commission, I retrieved my laptop from its case. I hadn't needed to use it recently, so I plugged the computer in just to make sure it worked. The screen lit up.

You're alive! I thought.

Soon I was checking e-mail. I stopped cold. There was a message from the clinic I'd been waiting to hear from. I opened the e-mail with hope soaring within me like a graceful albatross riding updrafts from Southern Ocean waves, riding them for literally thousands of miles across gray desolation and through frightening Antarctic storms. But as I read the terse note from the administrator, my fleeting sense of hope vanished in an instant. Rejected. Again.

How long is this going to go on? I wondered. *How long can I go on?*

I logged off and closed the lid of the laptop. I scooped Tweetie up and sat with her purring in my lap. My beloved cat was seemingly oblivious to the fury of the storm outside or to the storm of pain, frustration, anger, and despair roiling within my very essence. With the electric stimulation from the brain electrodes, my tremors are under control. The problem is that I can't speak clearly or quickly because the electrical impulses over the years have interfered with the speech center of my brain. My speech deteriorates when I'm tired or stressed. I can't just say, "I'm tired." It comes out, "*I-mm tie-eeerd.*" It's enormously frustrating, I can tell you that.

When potential employers hear about my Parkinson's disease and my deep brain stimulation that controls it, they run screaming from the room. Of course, they never say my condition is why they won't hire me. They don't want to get sued. I know my condition is exactly why I'm struggling and have struggled to work in my profession since 1994, and the discrimination just wears me down.

Imagine trying to talk with someone, your mind every bit as sharp as it was before you came down with Parkinson's disease, and yet you can't get the words out. It's difficult to express complex thoughts, and yet the thoughts are right there in my mind. I know what I want to say. I just can't express myself the way people without Parkinson's can. When I'm trying to get a point across, the individuals sitting across from me often start raising their voices, as if I'm deaf, which I'm not, and they lean close and start speaking very slowly. Like I'm stupid as well as deaf. They treat me like I'm a baby who doesn't know the language. Imagine how that would make you feel? Now imagine trying to serve geriatric patients. Now give a whirl at imagining trying to order your favorite meal at the Outback from a harried twenty-year-old waitress, or talking with a cop who has just pulled you over for speeding.

My patients understand what I'm going through better than most. Some of them are hard of hearing, so they know what it's like to be caught in a world where the spoken word is a challenge. Some of them are visually impaired, so they understand what it's like to be dislodged from a world that is built for the sighted. Some of them are suffering from the onset of dementia of the Alzheimer's type. They may not understand my condition, but they look at me with compassion. They all want my help in evaluating their conditions and making the proper recommendations that I believe as their physician will improve the quality of their lives. I've always said, being a good doctor is all about being a good listener. To treat an illness requires the physician to understand fully what the patient is going through. I'm a good listener, and I'm a good geriatrician. In a way, perhaps it was providence that I chose this field. If I were a psychologist or psychiatrist reliant on the spoken word, I'd have been out of luck.

The lights flickered on and off for a split second. The thunder and lightning were practically simultaneous. I couldn't get a "one Mississippi" out before the next round. The storm was right over my head, and it was also deep in my heart and soul.

5

When Wendy returned home after visiting her family over the Christmas holiday, I got the sense that a decision had been made. I didn't know what it was at the time. She became increasingly distant and we quarreled more often, if that was even possible. I would ask her what was wrong, and she would say we didn't have enough money. She would say she didn't like the way things were turning out between us. She didn't like how her life was turning out either. I honestly wonder how many of us really do think our lives are what we'd hoped for, but philosophically speaking I guess it doesn't really matter. Our lives are what they are. We can make changes. We can work toward a new horizon. In the final analysis, though, we have to play the cards we're dealt, and that's it. As the old saying goes, our lives aren't a dress rehearsal. Our lives are all we have, until we unwillingly cash out from the roulette table.

As I sat in a comfortable chair and listened to the wind trying to blow the roof off my old townhome, I recalled those tumultuous times. I recalled my confusion and fright. "But I don't know what's happening to me!" I'd say when Wendy and I fought into the wee hours of the morning before we both had to rub the sleep from our eyes and get to work. "I'm trying to find out! We have to find out together so we can beat this."

She'd say she was stressed out, and then she'd walk away from me. She sometimes even left me alone in our bed and sat up for hours drinking coffee at the kitchen table. At first, I'd get up and go into the kitchen to talk with her. After awhile it was like talking to a Sphinx. A black polished entity of unimaginable power over me. After awhile it just wasn't worth it. I stayed in bed and let her stew in her own juices while I stewed in mine.

As the Texas winter waned, I was referred to a neurologist, Dr. George Harrison. I hoped for answers at last.

"No worries, Dr. C," the neurologist said. "I know what you've got."

"What's that?"

"You have a benign essential familial tremor."

"Oh," I said. I had a vague idea of what that was, but I wanted a far more detailed explanation, which the doctor provided.

"I'll prescribe you some medicine—primidone and propranolol—that should take care of it," he said. "It's really nothing to worry much about."

I got up from the examination table and shook his hand. "Thanks, Doctor Harrison. The symptoms have been getting worse. I hope I can get some relief."

The neurologist stroked his chin and looked pensive for a few moments. He was a lanky guy about six feet tall with short blond hair cut in an almost military style. "I noticed you seem to be having trouble staying coordinated when you walk," he said. "But it's the tremor that's most troublesome, isn't it?"

I said it was. I also told him I was having trouble sleeping, that I was sweating more than usual, and that sometimes it was hard to swallow. I didn't mention that I was deeply and profoundly depressed.

"Well, let's see how you do on the meds. We can always do an electromagnetic nerve conduction study to see what's going on, but I'd like to hold off on that," he said. "There's probably no need to get into all that."

I agreed. After all, I was a geriatrician. I was not a neurologist. Neurology was reviewed extensively and I still have my notes from my professors in the VA. However, I had already begun reading up on neurological diseases. I guess it was the "doctor heal thyself" syndrome. I guess I had already started to mistrust the people who were supposed to be caring for me, the medical professionals who were supposed to know more than I did about matters of the brain. The more I learned, the more it seemed to me that I was suffering from young-onset, tremor dominant Parkinson's disease. Still, I deferred to the experts. Most patients do, and for good reason. Yet, ever since I'd started having health problems, I'd felt like I'd been plunged down the black rabbit hole in *Alice in Wonderland*.

Nothing in my medical training had prepared me to sit on the opposite side of the physician's desk. Nothing had prepared me for the frustration of the medical system, the interminable waiting for test results, the indifference of nurse receptionists, the maze of insurance company policies, the complete lack of compassion for the patient. It's all push 'em on through as fast as possible, like cars on an assembly line. In a way, it was a bit like being swept up in the prison system. You lose all control over your own destiny.

In retrospect, that first neurosurgeon's misdiagnosis wasn't all that surprising. Sadly, many cases of essential tremor, as it's called today, are misdiagnosed as Parkinson's disease, and many cases of Parkinson's disease are misdiagnosed as ET. Both involve tremors in the body. However, the two conditions are quite different. For one thing, ET is eight times more common than Parkinson's disease, according to studies from the International Essential Tremor Foundation. Had the doctor known more about ET, he would have asked if the tremors occurred mostly when my right foot was at rest. Mine did, but with ET tremors seldom occur when the body or limb is at rest. Tremors occur when you are moving. That would've been an immediate tip off for an astute physician.

My doctor also didn't pick up on the major clue about my increasing difficulty in walking in a normal way. Walking and balance problems known as Ataxia are uncommon with ET, whereas they are a major symptom of Parkinson's disease. Further, with ET the tremors occur in both sides of the body as soon as symptoms present. Tremors with Parkinson's disease start on one side of the body and spread to both sides of the body, slowly sapping your coordination in nearly every muscle in all your limbs. It even kills the muscle control in your face, so you end up looking really strange. You end up not being able to talk right. You end up seeming to be half human, except in your head and in your soul you are the same person you were before the horrid disease decided to call your body home. I think that is perhaps the biggest torture of them all, the being trapped inside a body that seems intent on killing the very essence of your humanity.

Another clue the doctor missed was my family history. Only 10 percent of people with Parkinson's have a family history of the disease, putting me in a very rare group. As I've said, my mother died of a fall while suffering from advanced Parkinson's. On the other hand, roughly 50 percent of patients with ET have it in their family histories, which is why the affliction was once often called "familial" or "hereditary" essential tremor. Had he asked, I would have said my mom had Parkinson's. He might have thought twice about his diagnosis. At least I might have had a fighting chance if he had asked more questions instead of jumping to an easy conclusion.

Even today diagnosing Parkinson's disease isn't like diagnosing a common cold. Very early on, an MRI should be done to determine whether the person suffering from symptoms common to Parkinson's disease is free of a brain tumor that could cause similar symptoms. To further complicate matters, Parkinson's is often mistaken for Wilson's disease as well as essential tremor. The newest available lab test, a dopa pet scan, can show reduced production of dopamine, which in turn can give credence to a correct diagnosis of Parkinson's. If possible, assessment should be undertaken at a Morris K. Udall Center of Excellence in Parkinson's disease Research.

These centers were developed in honor of former Congressman Morris K. Udall of Utah. Udall was elected to the U.S. House of Representatives in 1961 in a special election to replace his brother Stewart, who left the position to become President John F. Kennedy's Secretary of the Interior. Representative Udall was diagnosed with Parkinson's in 1979. He remained active in Congress until his retirement in May 1991. He died in 1998 after a long battle with the disease. On November 13, 1997, the president of the United States signed the Morris K. Udall Parkinson's Disease Research Act of 1997 into law.

That same year, the National Institute of Neurological Disorders and Stroke (NINDS) released a Request for Applications to establish the first Morris K. Udall Centers of Excellence in Parkinson's disease Research. The mission of the NINDS is to reduce the burden of neurological disease—a burden borne by every age group, by every segment of society, and by people all over the world. As a part of this mission, the NINDS supports basic, translational and clinical research on Parkinson's disease, a devastating and complex neurodegenerative disorder that progressively impairs the control of purposeful movement. Udall centers utilize a multidisciplinary research approach to elucidate the fundamental causes of Parkinson's as well as to improve the diagnosis and treatment of patients with Parkinson's and related neurodegenerative disorders. There was only one such center in Texas, and, regrettably, I didn't avail myself of the experts there from the outset.

In the mid-1990s, less was known about Parkinson's disease and essential tremor. Great progress has been made in treating both conditions, though we still have a long way to go. Stem-cell research could move things along toward an eventual cure for Parkinson's disease, but the political and moral posturing regarding the use of stem cells in clinical research in this country continues to stand in the way. Ultimately, embryonic stem-cell research due to the toti potential cell line development will lead to a permanent cure for idiopathic Parkinson's disease and many other neurodegenerative diseases of the brain and peripheral nervous system.

After more than ten years, the Morris K. Udall Centers of Excellence Program continues to forge a strong and innovative path in Parkinson's research. Areas of study include the identification and characterization of candidate and disease-associated genes, examination of neurobiological mechanisms, establishment of improved Parkinson's disease models, development and testing of potential therapeutics, and other novel avenues of clinical research. The centers continue to create and foster an environment that enhances the research effectiveness of investigators in a multidisciplinary setting, utilizing specialized methods relevant to the study of this disorder. NINDS is committed to continuing and enhancing the tradition of scientific excellence fostered by the Udall centers, and it will continue efforts to strengthen the program in coming years.

As I look back, I remain angry that the misdiagnosis left me with no relief whatsoever, even if I can intellectually understand why the doctor made a big mistake in thinking I had essential tremor. The medicines my first neurosurgeon prescribed didn't help. My symptoms worsened, and I finally sought the advice of one of the best neurologists in the country, a renowned physician by the name of Dr. H. Leonard. I did not receive a referral for the appointment from my existing physician, which meant my insurance company would not cover the cost of the visit. I had to pay out of pocket for the consultation. At that point, I was desperate for answers. I would've paid almost anything to get to the bottom of what was happening and to make the symptoms go away.

Wendy reluctantly accompanied me on the long drive. We said little to each other, despite my feeble attempts to make pleasant small talk about the scenery and the weather. I'd point out cows grazing in a pasture, and she would simply shoot me a look that said, "Get real." I was glad she was with me anyway, even if she was behaving like a cow's ass. I was so glad the tension that seemed always present between us didn't matter. I needed and wanted her support. I wanted her to feel the same hope that I did. I felt that the many months of agony might be over, that the doctor would know what was wrong with me, and that he might be able to prescribe an effective treatment. Then we could move on with our lives and repair the damage all the stress, the medical condition, and the loss of the job in California had caused in our once happy marriage.

I grew more and more excited as we entered the modern teaching hospital, its grounds immaculate, its architecture impressive, its orderlies, nurses, and physicians all business. I checked in, signed the forms, and furnished my credit card. I was told to wait. Wendy and I sat staring straight ahead on a sofa. She eventually picked up a women's magazine and began reading. Soon a nurse called my name and I was ushered into an examination room. A neurological fellow at the hospital sat down with me. I described my symptoms and the ineffective treatments. We spent about an hour together.

"I'm sorry, Dr. C, but I have to say I think you have idiopathic Parkinson's disease," the fellow said.

I was speechless for a long moment. Even though I'd begun to suspect I had Parkinson's, the reality of it hit me hard. It was like getting punched in the gut. The disease is incurable and progressive. I knew that at the time. The disease can disable you. I knew that too. The disease can destroy your life, if you let it. Mercifully, I didn't know that. I didn't consciously think about the fact that Mr. Parkinson's was already dismantling my life one stone at a time.

"Is there a treatment?" I asked. "I've been reading up on Parkinson's just in case it turned out I have it. It seems like there's no set treatment."

"There isn't. Every patient's symptoms are a little different. You're dealing with the brain. We don't fully understand how and why the brain works, not even with decades of advanced study. We do know that every brain is different, almost like a fingerprint. It's as unique as the individual is." The neurological fellow paused. He wrote something down on my chart. "There are treatments. Drugs. Physical therapy. I'll let Dr. Leonard know what the screening turned up. He'll be with you in a few minutes, okay?"

I swallowed hard and nodded.

Doctor Leonard came in a short time later and told me about treatments. For decades, the main course of action was, and largely still is, to slow the progression of the disease and reduce the symptoms through drug regimens. One of the most common drugs is called levodopa, or L-Dopa for short. The drug is supposed to help replace lost dopamine, which Parkinson's sucks from your brain as it kills off the cells you need to coordinate movement, or even to smile without looking like a weird jack-o-lantern. The loss of dopamine in turn causes a loss of communication between your brain and your muscles. L-Dopa is supposed to amp up the communication between your brain and your muscles, almost as if you had a drill sergeant with a loud public address system shouting messages from your head down.

"Right foot! Forward . . . *march!* Hand! Stop shaking, soldier! *Ten hut!*"

The problem with the drug is that as the disease progresses you can suffer from abrupt involuntary muscle movements, sleepiness and lethargy, vivid nightmares when you do fall asleep, visual and auditory hallucinations, and confusion. As Dr. Leonard told me about all this, I felt a sinking sensation in my stomach, but I also felt like I was a drowning man being thrown a life ring. I was ready for just about anything that would make the worsening symptoms take a permanent vacation to Tahiti. My life was falling apart. Stone by stone the wall was coming down, and the hordes were at the gate. I needed some heavy artillery, and I needed it fast.

There are also drugs called dopamine receptor agonists, drugs like pergolide and bromocriptine, to name just a few. These drugs are frequently taken in conjunction with L-Dopa, creating a potent concoction. Selegeline, amantadine, and anti-cholinergics are also commonly prescribed drugs for the treatment of Parkinson's disease. Of course, I didn't know that at the time. I knew very little about Parkinson's. My head was swimming and spinning with the new reality that was thrust upon me. I was now not only down Alice's rabbit hole, I was caught in a raging river and being carried downstream toward Niagara Falls in a leaky wooden barrel.

As I listened to Dr. Leonard, it became clear that the way ahead was going to require a cocktail of powerful drugs that would hopefully subdue the beast rearing up inside my brain. Nutritional supplements and physical therapy would also play a big part in my treatment plan. The physical therapy made perfect sense. After all, Parkinson's is a disease that attacks muscle coordination. I just wondered if all this crap would work. Even then I had my doubts.

I couldn't help but think, *Why me? What did I ever do to deserve this? Why, God, have you forsaken me?* But, then, those thoughts did not last long. I was a geriatrician. I dealt with and still deal with people who have every right to ask the same damn question, and who face their realities with a degree of grace and courage I could and can only admire to the greatest depths of my very being. I did not bask in self-pity for long.

"Well, uh, thank you, Dr. Leonard. I think."

"I know it's a lot to process right now, but trust me. It's not the end of the world. You can get through this. Lots of people do," Dr. Leonard said.

I sighed. "Yes, I suppose you're right."

Dr. Leonard's eyes shone with compassion and wisdom. It was the first I'd seen since I'd gone down the churning vortex of a very indifferent medical system. I could see that he empathized with me. I could see that he understood that the news he was confirming would forever change my life, and quite decidedly not for the better.

"Well, let's see," he said, obviously trying to sound cheerful. "Yes, I know a very good neurologist in your area. A Dr. Clarence Powers. He knows his stuff. You'll be in good hands with him. I'll have my receptionist set up an appointment with him."

"Okay, Dr. Leonard!" I said. I was trying to sound cheerful too. I felt anything but. "Sooner rather than later would be good."

"Of course!"

Dr. Leonard whisked out of the examination room, and I whisked to the front desk. Wendy was absorbed in her magazine. She didn't even look up. I made arrangements to see Dr. Powers, and then I walked over to my wife and sat down next to her. She looked up, set her magazine down on the coffee table in front of her, and reached over and took my hand.

"How'd you do, Simon?" she asked.

"Not so good."

Wendy looked crestfallen.

"Come on, let's get out of here," I said, squeezing her hand back. "I'll tell you all about it the car."

I thought she was going to cry, and for some strange reason I was glad about that. Not that she was on the verge of tears, but because she seemed suddenly to care more than she had before.

"Okay," she said. She stood and straightened her hair.

"Okay, then," I said. I stood up too. "Are you hungry, honey?" I asked.

Wendy didn't answer me. Instead, we walked silently out of Dr. Leonard's office and back out into the parking garage adjacent to the hospital. The sun shone through the rectangular concrete openings on the fourth level, bathing the parked cars in subdued light. Outside, the world bustled by as if it didn't have a care. The sky gleamed a brilliant blue. The sound Wendy's heels made on the concrete echoed off the dirty walls. I suddenly had the feeling that I'd just been launched into outer space without a capsule.

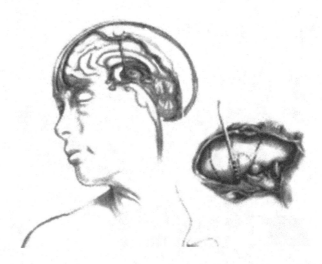

DBS illustration (c) Medtronic Corporation. 2013

6

The side effects from the drug cocktail began shortly after I started taking L-Dopa and other meds, kicking off a battle that would last for seven very long and devastating years. For a brief period, L-Dopa gave me relief and I was absolutely euphoric about it. It's difficult to describe what it's like to have uncontrollable tremors. Your feet, arms, and hands twitch as the muscles receive conflicting messages from the brain and go haywire. You can grab your hands or feet to hold them still, but it doesn't work. So, you're left shaking until you want to scream. Over time it can really drive you nuts, and you'll try anything to make it stop.

Imagine my disappointment when L-Dopa gradually gave me less and less relief. Imagine my agony at having to put up with the side effects with little to show for it. L-Dopa is highly effective for many patients suffering from Parkinson's. It can reduce symptoms and slow the advance of the disease. I was deeply depressed when I concluded that I didn't seem to be one of the lucky ones who could benefit much from L-Dopa. Later, I tried Stalevo, with similarly disappointing results. I simply could not tolerate these medications in doses high enough to do significant good.

Instead of not being able to sleep well at night, the medications made me drowsy during the day. I never felt rested. Worse yet, I began to experience the slight emergence of hallucinations that gradually worsened as my neurologist tried new combinations of drugs. At first, I didn't know what was happening to me when I saw flashes of things that weren't there. My depression deepened still more, and prescribing drugs to combat it proved challenging because some anti-depressants can react badly with drugs taken to reduce the symptoms of Parkinson's disease.

As the hallucinations increased, I thought I might be losing my mind, but deep inside me a voice cried out for me to seek help. A voice of hope remained strong. I went back to Dr. Powers, a short middle-aged man with dark brown hair and deep blue eyes. He had that arrogant way about him that I've seen in many physicians, especially neurologists, and it had irked me from the very start when we'd first met three years earlier after Dr. Leonard diagnosed me as a Parkinson's case.

"These drugs are making me hallucinate," I said.

"Nonsense," he said, his arms folded across his chest. "No one hallucinates with this treatment."

"Well, I am hallucinating. I keep seeing paisley elephants. Sometimes they're pink. They look a lot like Dumbo. One second they're there, and the next second they're gone. I'm losing my sense of balance more rapidly now. I think the meds are making things worse."

"Perhaps you have an abnormal brain," he said. His facial expression was deadly serious. He was not joking at all.

I stared at him for a long moment, trying to control my temper. "Well, I don't agree with you, doctor. My brain's perfectly normal, except it has Parkinson's living inside it."

"I'm just saying that hallucinations are practically unheard of on these drugs, so something strange is going on. I'd rather not take you off the meds. We haven't toughed it out long enough yet."

I took a deep breath and glanced up at the ceiling. "Not long enough? How long is long enough?"

"Let's just wait it out a little longer, okay? If we don't see improvement soon we'll just have to try something else," Dr. Powers said.

I didn't want to hear that, but he was my doctor and I deferred to him on the matter. "Okay," I said, "we'll do it your way for now."

Dr. Powers smiled and said, "Trust me. The meds will work. Just give the new cocktail time."

I wasn't so sure. In addition to the hallucinations, I suffered from paranoia. I felt afraid and anxious all the time. Sometimes I'd get dizzy and have to sit down. The meds also made me break out in rashes whenever I was out in the sun due to photo toxicity. There's a lot of sunshine in Texas, so this was a real problem. I briefly contemplated moving to Seattle.

I left Dr. Powers's office feeling just awful as I drove back home to an empty apartment. My divorce from Wendy had recently been finalized after dragging on for three vitriolic years, and as part of the settlement she got possession of my four beloved cats. The day I had to collect them and bring them to a veterinarian, where she would pick them up, was one of the worst in my life. They were like my children. They had served as steadfast companions from the day I retrieved them from the animal shelter.

Some nurses at a clinic I was working at had fed them, and as strays they kept coming back for more food. The administrator of the clinic had them taken to the pound, where they were about to be put down. I rescued them. Now they were gone. That was worse than the financial settlement I'd been forced into. It didn't matter to the judge that Wendy had abandoned me only weeks after I'd been diagnosed with Parkinson's disease. I came home one day to find a note on our little bar that said she was leaving me with words to the effect that she hadn't signed on for life with a sick guy.

The only good thing that had happened recently to offset the loss of my cats was my meeting Monique at the correctional facility where I worked two days a week covering for the medical director. Like my father, she was steeped in French culture, having maternal roots in France. She spoke the language fluently. Like Wendy, she was blonde, had blue eyes, and was blessed with a figure right out of Victoria Secret. She was a Director of Nursing nurse at the jail, and we worked together upon occasion. It didn't take long for us to become more than just friends. It didn't take long for me to fall head over heels in love with her. I thought at last that I'd found a soul mate, a person who would stand with me as I went through my personal combat with Mr. P, as I'd taken to calling my uninvited cerebral guest. I'd proposed to her and she'd said yes. By taking Monique on I was also committing to take care of her son. I didn't mind. I'd always wanted kids.

In the summer of 1998, the same year I met Monique and fell in love with her, my reaction to the meds worsened further. One day that summer forced a major change in my life. I'd picked Monique up after work and we were driving along in my silver Jeep Cherokee. Bob Dylan's "Dignity" was playing on the radio. Suddenly, paisley and pink elephants flashed across my field of vision, distracting me for a moment. The hoofs made a loud bump-gee-bump noise. I couldn't hear Bob Dylan.

"Oh, my God! Simon!" Monique screamed.

I was speeding and about to slam into a tractor-trailer that didn't yield.

"Simon!"

I spun the wheel and hit the brakes while still seeing the damnable elephants, and I barely missed colliding with the truck. Monique was breathing hard, and so was I as I slowed the Jeep down. Evidently satisfied for the moment, the elephants sauntered back to the bizarre savannah of my troubled mind. I tried to comfort Monique, but to no avail. Later that night, I sat alone thinking about what had happened. We both could have been killed. I was at a loss as to what to do about the meds and my resident elephants, but I made the decision to quit driving from that point on. I'd bear the extra expense of taking a cab to work. I couldn't live with guilt if Dumbo showed up at precisely the wrong moment and I caused a fatal car wreck, killing an innocent driver or passenger in the other vehicle.

My relationship with Monique deteriorated along with my condition. It was getting harder and harder to hold down a job. My future looked dim. Monique and I began to fight more frequently, especially after we moved in together. The arguments were often about money, but not always. It seemed we could battle over just about anything. Her jabs about not feeling able to deal with my Parkinson's and my co-dependency really hurt. They reminded me of what Wendy used to say to me. At times, she called the sheriff on me, and I had to deal with the cops and explain that we were merely having an argument, that there was no domestic physical abuse going on.

Stress is a killer for anybody, but for a person suffering from Parkinson's disease, it's particularly harmful. Stress magnifies the symptoms and increases the progression of the disease. I was having limited nursing care at the time, and in a moment of lapsed judgment I allowed one of the nurses to seduce me. The nurse then told Monique, and that was the end of my love affair with a very seductive and volatile woman. My indiscretion was wrong, but we are all only human. We all have our faults. We all make mistakes that we regret later. Through circumstance and happenstance I found myself alone once again, gradually declining into a state of utter despair.

Dawn did not bring an end to the procession of violent thunderstorms pummeling San Antonio and surrounding communities. I stood looking out my patio windows at the whirls of driving rain. Darkness and fury cloaked the city. The ambiance matched my foul mood as I thought about the most recent rejection from yet another clinic. I wondered what I was going to do if I could not find work soon. It seemed like the deck had been stacked against me for nearly a decade, and I guessed that it truly had been, largely through no fault of my own. When you are hit with a serious incurable disease right out of the blue, it can throw you into turmoil. It can tip everything normal in your life upside down, and it's hard to get right side up again.

Sighing, I turned away from the window and stalked over to the TV. I turned it on and sat down, leaning forward in mild shock as I watched the live coverage of the storm. The National Weather Service had issued seven flood warnings, and eight additional flash food warnings for the area. The news footage showed roads completely submerged in the continuing driving rain. In some places only the roofs of abandoned cars were visible, and in others the cars were completely inundated. The water lapped at the bottom edge of stop signs. Storefronts downtown were under the water. People living along the San Antonio River were being asked to evacuate their homes. Residents outside of the evacuation zone were ordered to stay put. I, for one, had no intention of setting foot outside. The winds rattled the windows and roared between the townhomes in the subdivision. The thunder growled. The rain beat down without any indication of letting up.

"What a damn mess," I whispered.

Suddenly, the very wet newscaster interrupted his report on a woman who had drowned when her car was swept against a culvert to say a possible tornado had touched down at six o'clock, just a few minutes earlier, near the Rolling Oaks Mall. Three tornado warnings had already been issued. I wondered if it might not be so bad if a twister came and blissfully carried me away to Oz.

7

Years passed. The new millennia arrived without a hitch, putting to rest the Y2K fears that all the computers in the world would go bonkers because they assumed dates began with a nineteen, as opposed to a twenty. Terrorists flew hijacked planes into the World Trade Center and the Pentagon, and forever changed the way Americans viewed the Middle East and their own sense of security at home. My own personal battle with Parkinson's disease raged on with little change, except I finally took myself off the brain poison Dr. Powers prescribed. It truly was a case of "Doctor, heal thyself." The symptoms from Parkinson's disease persisted, of course, but at least I got rid of Dumbo and his rowdy friends, the paranoia, and my photo toxicity. I could also drive again, which was a relief and a necessity.

Still, life was a struggle. Doing simple things like stepping into an elevator, getting in and out of the car, dressing, buying groceries, making dinner, cleaning the house (I eventually hired a cleaning lady), and so much more became an effort. I was not alone in this. While not every patient goes through all the stages of the disease, many of us share symptoms and challenges in common.

Life as you knew it before Parkinson's fades into oblivion. As the disease progresses, all of your functional mobility is impacted. Hand movements become awkward, your steps become smaller, and the volume of your voice drops. It's even hard to lift your feet, and serious injury from falling becomes a real issue. Your facial expressions are minimized, giving you a blank robot-like look that puts people off. We humans communicate with our facial expressions, so losing that ability cuts you off from the rest of the world even more. Swallowing is impaired. Taking pills and eating is difficult and time consuming. Your saliva builds up in your mouth, and there's little you can do to stop yourself from drooling like an infant. Lemon triggers the swallowing reflex, so lots of us like to put lemon in our drinks, or we suck on lemon lollipops or lemon drops.

Although there is no scientific evidence to back it up, many Parkinson's patients like me do seem to benefit from certain nutritional supplements. There are too many of them to list, but I found that CoQ-10 and Ubiquinol helped me during this period. Treating my sleep apnea lessened the stress on my body, allowing me to enter restorative deep REM sleep. Physical and spiritual therapy can play a part in coping with Parkinson's as well. The idea behind physical therapy is that movement through specific exercises will strengthen the muscles. It's definitely a "use it or lose it" proposition. Spiritual faith can decrease your depression. At least it did for me. In short, since the meds were essentially reducing me to a human wreck, I pursued a battery of other methods to reduce the symptoms and slow the relentless progression of the disease.

Spiritual faith represented a key turning point in my life with Parkinson's. I'd always been a practicing Episcopal, and in my dark time I leaned more heavily on Jesus as a source of peace and hope. I am a member of the Order of St. Luke, which was founded in 1932, in St. Luke's Church, in San Diego, California, by the Reverend John Gayner Banks and his wife, Ethel Tulloch Banks. It was started as a Christian fellowship of clergy and lay people interested in sharing experiences of Jesus's healing ministry. Their vision was to draw all those involved in various healing ministries under the umbrella of a worldwide Christian healing fellowship, which would be based on the four Gospels of Jesus Christ. In 1953, it was incorporated in the state of California as The International Order of St. Luke the Physician.

The twentieth century saw an awakening around the world to the tremendous resources of God's healing power. God's power to heal is available to all of us, not only through scientific medicine, but through believing prayer. As a result of this awakening, the Reverend Banks and his wife were inspired to organize The Order of St. Luke. Their vision was one of inclusion that would invite people of all faiths from around the world to join them.

As the fellowship grew, a monthly, two-page newsletter was sent to all members. With further growth, the newsletter became a magazine. After prayer for guidance, the founding group decided to call the magazine *Sharing*. The first issue of *Sharing* was mailed in 1937, and the magazine has been in print ever since. Today the Order of Saint Luke the Physician has over seventy-five hundred members in North America, including lay people, clergy, and medical professionals. They believe that Christian healing and competent medical practices are not averse to one another but, rather, are complimentary. From the time the Order of St. Luke was founded, our members have devoted themselves to conducting healing missions at home and abroad, lecturing, teaching, and praying for those who are ill in body and soul—everywhere inspiring new members to join our healing fellowship. As a result, today chapters of many different denominations exist throughout the world.

Perhaps more than at any other time in history, our world is presently torn with bodies and souls that are sick and broken, so the task before us is far from finished. God's call to all of us is abundantly clear, and He awaits our joyful and enthusiastic response. Each one of us has some special healing gift to offer, and the Order of St. Luke is committed to helping each one of us realize that gift. For me, in my period of loneliness and sorrow, the bright light of Jesus led the way to a profound change in my life for the better.

After I took myself off the many of the toxic meds, Dr. Powers mentioned a procedure called deep brain stimulation (DBS). I'd never heard of it.

"DBS has been getting a lot of attention in the medical press," Dr. Powers said. "It's been around for quiet awhile in one form or another, but it's now being done as a treatment that is said to reduce or eliminate most of the effects of Parkinson's disease."

I perked up. "Really?" I asked. "Did you say *eliminate* the symptoms?"

"Reduce is the better word. And it works on most symptoms. DBS is very effective at stopping tremors, for example. It's a risky procedure, though. It involves open craniotomy and neurosurgery. The FDA only just approved DBS several months ago, which is why I haven't told you about it before. It wasn't an option here in the U.S., until now."

I nodded, said I understood. We talked some more, and then we were done with the appointment. For the first time, I left Dr. Powers's office with a tiny ray of hope instead of complete frustration and despair, but I also had more questions. Zillions, in fact.

I immediately began researching deep brain stimulation, and what I discovered truly fascinated and intrigued me, stoking my hope for relief at last. It turned out that two physicians, Benabid and Pollak, leaders of a team of research neurosurgeons and neurologists based in Grenoble, France, had been experimenting with DBS and had revealed groundbreaking findings in a paper published in 1987. I learned that the procedure does not cut the brain, but rather electrically stimulates "target" areas inside the brain (thalamus, subthalamic nucleus, and globus pallidus), blocking electrical signals from those areas that would otherwise cause tremors, rigidity, stiffness, slowed movement, and walking problems.

In the 1990s, a common surgical procedure called a thalamotomy was used to combat the symptoms of Parkinson's disease. It involved destroying a small section of the brain called the thalamus, which controls involuntary movements in the body. The procedure was risky and sometimes did more damage than good. It looked to me like DBS marked a major surgical improvement, and time has proven me right. In 1993, the same French team of physicians introduced subthalamic DBS, allowing for additional targeting of areas within the brain.

Today, DBS is the most rapidly expanding field in neurosurgery, even branching out to include applications to treat certain psychiatric disorders, according to a recent study from Harvard University. It is now an accepted treatment for Parkinson's disease, essential tremor, and dystonia. It replaced the thalamotomy and bilateral posteroventral pallidotomy, another common surgery for Parkinson's disease in the 1990s that involved creating a scar in the globus pallidus portion of the brain to stop disruptive electrical nerve signals that caused some of the more odious symptoms. The surgeon created the scar by freezing the area with liquid nitrogen circulating inside a hollow probe inserted through a hole in the skull while the patient was awake. The risks associated with these surgeries were such that I did not seriously consider them. While most symptoms are dramatically reduced with DBS, if it's done right, Parkinson's patients generally still need to take medications such as L-Dopa, but in far smaller doses. This in turn reduces the likelihood of adverse side effects like the ones I suffered from.

The DBS system is ingenious. Today, the neurosurgeon does what is called brain mapping to identify the target areas within the brain where electrical nerve signals are generating the symptoms, such as tremors. This is done using magnetic resonance imaging (MRI) or computed tomography (CT scan). Once the brain is mapped, a thin insulated wire, or lead, is inserted through a hole in the skull and implanted in the target area within the brain. The tip of the lead, also called an electrode, is stuck in the precise spot where the disruptive nerve signals are coming from. A longer wire, much like an extension cord, is run under the scalp, the skin of the neck, and the shoulder, and is then connected to a neurostimulator about the size of a stopwatch. The neurostimulator, or battery pack, is implanted under the skin in the area of the collarbone. When the system is in place, charges from the battery pack travel to the brain to zap the disruptive electrical nerve signals.

By the late spring of 2002, I was pretty much convinced that I should go for DBS. The problem was I didn't have insurance that would pay for it, and the cost to me would run close to seventy grand. Another problem was that the procedure was brand-new in the United States and neurosurgeons like Dr. Gauge were still working out the kinks. I knew if I signed on for DBS that I was, in essence, agreeing to be one of the first Parkinson's patients in the country to try it. I would be a sort of human guinea pig. That didn't sit well with me, but the plague of the symptoms continued and I saw no other option. I'd tried everything since my diagnosis in 1995, with little success. If anything, the stress of my divorce and my breakup with Monique, the ongoing struggle to get and keep a job as a geriatrician, and the exhaustion from fighting the disease made my symptoms worse, not better or even stable.

I scheduled the operation with Dr. Gauge. Then I chickened out and cancelled. The idea of a surgeon drilling holes in my head to implant electrodes hooked up to a battery tucked inside my body frightened me. I wondered if the risks were worth it. Dr. Powers said precious little about the inherent risks of such surgery, but I found out what they were on my own. Infection, stroke, bleeding in the brain, paralysis, permanent damage to my voice, and double vision were the biggies. Of course, I could always die on the table too. That happens more often than you might think. I'd rolled the dice before with Parkinson's and came up with snake eyes, so I was understandably wary about going through with the DBS surgery. I prayed about the decision, and I finally sought the guidance of my minister in a local chapter of the Order of St. Luke.

As I sprawled in my bed with Tweetie at my side and listened to the rain falling, I recalled that momentous day so long ago now in the summer of 2002. The images flooded back to me like the swollen rivers and creeks running wild through the streets of San Antonio. It was as if I were back in my car driving to the church.

My hands trembled as I gripped the steering wheel and tried to concentrate on the road. Willing my hands to stop shaking wasn't enough. I was sadly used to the palsy. I sighed and turned on the radio, hoping to catch a Bob Dylan tune. I drove on under the blazing, brilliant South Texas sky, deeply conflicted about what to do. Depression settled over me like a heavy dark cloak. The day was beautiful, but I had a hard time appreciating it.

I drove on, and in a short while I reached the highway turnoff to the surface roads leading to my church. I'd turned to God for solace, and I had faith that the answer to my dilemma would come. I figured He was about the only trustworthy element in my reality at the time, a steady hand I could rely on for guidance and inner strength. I knew my faith would see me through these hard times. I was alone in the world with nobody to turn to for comfort or even to share my feelings with. My very life seemed to hang in the balance between bad and even worse. I desperately wanted to see positive change in my life, even if the change was incremental for the better in only small ways. By the sound of it, successful DBS surgery could bring monumental change for the good.

I pulled up to my Episcopal Church, a diminutive Gothic structure of limestone with parallel walls of Edwardian stain glass and well-kept grounds. I parked, got out of the car, and entered the building. My minister greeted me in the cool chapel ringed with a turret of the stained glass and the Ten Commandments. The sun shone through the stained-glass windows. The church was quiet, and I felt at peace, like I'd just come into port after an arduous voyage on a storm-tossed sea. We exchanged some small talk, and then I said, "I need your help. I need you to pray with me. I have a decision to make, and I don't know what to do."

"Come, Simon," he said, extending his hand, "sit with me and tell me how God can help."

We sat together in silence for a long moment. I heard my heart beating in my ears. I felt the familiar panic and fear wash in once again, but then it slackened and almost disappeared as I looked from my minister to the altar. I was in God's house, and I somehow knew that everything would be okay in spite of the great anguish and anxiety I had been feeling regarding whether or not to have the surgery.

My minister and I prayed together, and I felt the presence of the Holy Spirit. I felt strength pouring into my heart and soul when my minister anointed me. I told him I was ready, that I would have the procedure. We said goodbye. I walked to my car, feeling the hot Texas sun on my face. The tremors were still present, as always, but I dared to hope that I might soon find relief.

Back on the highway I drove in silence, lost in my own thoughts. Anxiety still lingered. How could it not? I was about to have brain surgery. I was about to have two electrodes inserted in my brain matter, not something you do on a whim. Not something you do at all, unless you feel you have no choice. As I drove home, I thanked Jesus for His sacrifices, for His wisdom, for His love and guidance. Suddenly, a drop of water splashed on the windshield. Then another and another fell. I looked up, and there wasn't even the wisp of a cloud in the clear blue sky. And yet the soothing, cleansing rain came, a sign from Jesus that at last I might be moving from the darkness into the light, that at last my life would have meaning again as I moved forward into a new day.

8

Dr. Gauge came to see me while I was being prepped for surgery. He looked calm, cool, and collected in his scrubs. He asked how I was holding up.

"Fine, I guess," I said, "but I'm going to need a baseball cap."

Dr. Gauge laughed. "Your hair will grow back fast. You'll see! You'll look just fine."

"I'm used to not looking just fine, so that'll be something," I mumbled.

"Okay, then," Dr. Gauge said. "I'll see you in there shortly."

Dr. Gauge walked out, the confidence oozing from him. I still had my misgivings about the surgery, but Jesus had led me to the decision to go forward. I had to trust in Jesus. I had to give myself a chance to regain a sense of calm and peace that I'd lost seven years earlier, or, actually, nearly eight years to the month when I first noticed the slight quivering in my right foot. It had been a long and torturous journey, and I hoped the painful trek would be over. I was also scared. I didn't know if I'd even wake up, or if I would be able to think, talk, or see straight if I did. I felt a little like a hapless lab rat about to get an experimental treatment, and in many ways that's exactly what I was.

"Are you ready, Dr. C?" the RN circulating operating room nurse with her star wars millennium falcon bandanna asked. "We've got to get you into the OR now."

I said I was, even though I wasn't sure about that at all.

A few minutes later, the IV margarita-like anesthesia running through the catheter in my left hand put me under, banishing the noise of the gurney, the hushed voices of the attending nurses, the announcements over the hospital public address system. The bright lights faded into nothing, and then I was gone. I ventured to another place far, far away deep in my mind. I don't know if I saw any bump-gee-bumping elephants. I don't know what I saw when I was under and Dr. Gauge placed a sort of frame over my bald head to provide exterior reference points for the drill for the CT guided reference points to the sub-thalamic nuclei. I didn't feel him peel back my scalp to expose the bare bone of my skull, nor did I hear the whir of the drill or feel the bit sink deep until the first site hole was completed. I didn't feel the tip of the electrode plunge into my brain tissue in the area where Dr. Gauge thought the tip should go. He was operating blind without the modern brain mapping we have today. The facility didn't have that as an option back then. Others did, but not this one. Dr. Gauge assured me that brain mapping wasn't required, that he knew what he was doing.

"Can you hear me, Simon?"

A strange garbled voice roused me and drew me back to the world outside my mind.

"Simon? Can you hear me?"

I realized the voice belonged to Dr. Gauge. I realized in terror that I was awake and still immobilized on the operating table. Intense bright light shone in my eyes, blinding me. The beep of the heart monitor, the sound of the oxygen pump, the meat-locker cold of the room, the strange sensation in my skull, it all pushed and shoved into my bleary consciousness. I fought back the panic. I fought back the terror.

"Simon, we had to bring you out," Dr. Gauge said. "Now, raise your right hand, okay?"

"Wh-what?"

"Simon, raise your right hand. I need to see that we've gotten rid of the tremor."

I felt sick, scared, and confused. What was I doing awake? Was the surgery over? I guessed that it wasn't based on the fact that I was strapped down on an operating table. I summoned all my will and raised my right hand. Above my right hand a saw Archangel Michael watching over me.

"Good, Simon! Excellent! Looks like we got it!"

I heard Dr. Gauge move closer. I knew he was looking at the holes in my head. I knew he was somehow looking inside my skull with sophisticated tiny cameras. The feeling of utter helplessness you get in a situation like that is impossible to describe. You have to live it. You have to have a man literally inside your head while you're conscious to fathom the unearthly sense of it all.

"Put him under again," Dr. Gauge said.

Seconds later, a wave of blackness washed over me, and I went back to the land far, far away in my mind. Then the next thing I knew I was awake in the recovery room, bursting into consciousness with a jolt, the kind of startling plunge back into reality that sometimes happens when you're lying in bed half asleep and then come fully awake in a flash. I knew I was in the the neurosurgery intensive care unit under close scrutiny just in case there were complications from the surgery. I had an IV drip I assumed was dispensing morphine mixed with saline. The machines around me whirred and purred and beeped.

"I see you're awake," said the RN. "How do you feel?" Tonight you will stay here, and if you are stable Dr. Old blood will let you go home.

As I continued to come to, the realization that the tremors were still there began to take hold. It was hard to think clearly, but it was obvious that the DBS hadn't worked. I panicked. I felt a little like a human martini shaker. That's how bad it was.

"N-n-nurse! My tremors! I still have tremors!"

She took my right hand in hers. "Why so you do!" she said, and walked quickly away.

"Nurse! Come back! The surgery didn't work!" I called as loudly as I could. In actuality, my voice was no louder than a raspy whisper.

I lay shaking in the bed. If anything, the tremors were worse than before. I couldn't believe what was happening. I couldn't understand it. I was more confused than anything else. I remained awake. Every time a nurse went by, I asked to see Dr. Gauge. In the end, it was the representative from the manufacturer of the DBS neurostimulator who came to see me. She was allowed into the

ICU as a sort of consultant or customer service clerk. She messed around with my activator, a device that controls the amount of electricity the battery sends to the electrodes in my head. It also has two voltage settings, high and low, and a battery-life indicator. When the battery gets low, the activator issues a silent alarm.

"Oh, my Lord! They didn't turn you on!" she said. "Well, for heavens sake! You have to be turned on for you to get the relief you need. Let's get you fired up right away, honey!"

The rep fiddled around with my activator and suddenly I felt the most amazing sensation I'd ever felt in my entire life. It was like someone had turned a switch, which, in fact, the rep had done just seconds before. One second I was shaking and in pain, and the next second the tremors simply ceased to bother me. If they were still there, I couldn't tell. The relief was heavenly, rapturous even. The electricity surging from my battery, up the wires running under my skin and scalp, and into the electrodes now stuck into my brain on both sides of my head were effectively jamming the signals that my nerve cells were sending to my muscles that caused the tremors. It was like one of those radar-jamming planes we use to cripple enemy air defense systems before we go in and blast all the bad guys. The tremor-causing signals were toast. It was incredible!

"I've got you set on A, which is the maximum functional voltage level," the rep said. "So, how do you feel now?"

"I, I, I can't believe it! *It's a miracle!*"

"I know. It's pretty amazing, isn't it? I see patients react like that all the time, and it's just wonderful! Just wonderful!"

71

"I don't feel the tremors anymore!"

"That's just great, honey! Now, like I said before. To make the battery last longer, you'll have to turn yourself down to the B setting at night before you go to bed. If you feel any tremors, they'll go away as you fall asleep. In the morning, you just turn yourself right back on at the A setting and you'll be good to go!" the rep said. "It's as simple as that!"

I was elated, but the surgery had taken a lot out of me. I was still groggy from the anesthesia and the pain meds. My eyes fluttered.

"You rest now, you hear? You came through just fine. You're going to be just peachy now. We'll check in with you after you're discharged just to make sure everything is okay," the rep said.

"Okay," I said.

"Bye now!" the rep said, and sashayed away.

I remained in the hospital until it was clear all had gone well, and then I drove myself home. The house was quiet and empty. I wanted to share my apparent victory over Parkinson's disease with someone, but my life was devoid of human companions, female or male. I think that was partially my fault. I can be a difficult person at times. Add an eight-year ordeal with an incurable disease, horrific side effects from drugs used to ineffectively treat the disease, chronic depression, a divorce, a failed engagement, unstable employment, and financial woes together and you've got the makings of trouble with any kind of new relationship. I tended to withdraw into myself, and although I was lonely it was a state of being I knew so well that it began to seem normal.

I think my lack of male and female companions then and now also stems from the nature of American society. In this electronic digital age with its Internet-based social media human interaction isn't done face-to-face as much as it was in the past. Everyone sits at a computer instead, or they send idiotic text messages on cell phones. The mobility of the culture means you don't put down roots in any single place. You move around. If you do make friends, the relationships are likely to be superficial at best. I don't and didn't blame my loneliness on the society, but I do believe the current age is conducive to isolation. It encourages narcissistic tendencies and a complete lack of empathy for others.

And then there is the impediment of my disease. Being around someone with Parkinson's can make the uninitiated feel uncomfortable. If I can't smile at you or convey emotion through facial expressions, it's going to be hard for you to connect with me on a personal level. You'll subconsciously think I'm not getting what you're trying to say, even if I so totally do get what you're saying. If I drool (I don't, by the way), it would embarrass you. If I shake (I don't since DBS), it will make you feel self-conscious. There's also the unease that comes from the very human response that wants to flee from sickness and death. The disabled and seriously ill of all types will tell you that making friends can present some interesting challenges.

So, I came home from that first DBS surgery in a celebratory mood. Looking in the mirror, my appearance was somewhat startling, what with the white bandages over the wounds and the baldness of my head. In spite of how I looked, I knew I'd just come through a watershed moment and that my life would never be the same again. I could start anew with a sense of calm that had eluded me since the autumn of 1994. I didn't care that I was now battery operated like some boat or plane in a toy store, or that every two to three years I'd have to have surgery to replace the battery when it neared the end of its life. I didn't care that I'd transformed into a strange version of Frankenstein's monster with electrodes jammed into my brain and wires running down my neck and shoulder to a power source that I would now rely on to keep the symptoms of my Parkinson's disease at bay. For me, the morph to robot man was worth every bit of the post-op pain I still felt. I believed I now had a fighting chance to get my life back, to find a new and better position, and possibly even begin a relationship with a woman that would actually work out.

The rain began to ease off some as Saturday morning progressed, but it was still steady, adding more water to an already flooding San Antonio. I had the TV on and listened as I made coffee and toast in the kitchen. Tweetie sat on the counter with me after she finished eating. She looked happy and content, and I couldn't help but smile at her while I went about making my simple meal. No microwaves for me. Those can turn off my neurostimulator. Security x-rays at airports can do the same, which is why flying is a real challenge for me. As I sat down to eat, I felt very tired, having slept little during the night, what with all the thunder, the water damage, the rejection from the clinic, and my overall somber mood. I figured I'd try to nap when I finished my coffee and toast.

Hell, I obviously wasn't going anywhere. Not in the middle of a raging storm.

All the local TV stations were covering the weather and flooding live, which wasn't surprising. I was no meteorologist, but it was plain to see that this event was rare indeed. This part of Texas doesn't receive a lot of rain, and yet it can at times when the weather gods conspire to get conditions just right for a real whopper. They had outdone themselves this time, and to get so much rain so fast was bound to cause plenty of trouble. Apparently, the water was so high the fire department had to deploy eight swift-water boats and had already made well over one hundred rescues, plucking people out of stranded vehicles and off the roofs of inundated homes. In one case, a municipal bus was swept away and firefighters needed a boat to save the three passengers and the driver.

As I sipped my coffee and watched the mayhem unfold on TV, I thought back to October 1998 when a similar flood occurred. More than thirty inches of rain fell in a two-day period, killing more than thirty people as the Guadalupe and San Antonio Rivers overflowed their banks.

What is it about natural disasters that captivates with such effect? I wondered.

I was sure that people all over the city were glued to their TV sets just like me. I was sure that people were sorry for the additional two victims who had died earlier in the day, and for all the homeowners and business owners who had lost everything in the floods and fires. Yet, human nature is such that we rejoice in the fact that we were spared, that the horrible thing didn't happen to us. It is the same when it comes to nasty diseases. You'll hear friends chat in a diner, and it becomes clear.

Friend one: "Say, did you hear Betty Lou has cancer?"

Friend two: "No way!"

Friend one: "Yeah, she's in chemo. Not doing so hot either."

Friend two: "Oh, my, what a shame. Terrible. Just terrible."

Friend one: "You hear LeBron James and the Miami Heat kicked ass on the Spurs?"

Friend two: "We'll get 'em in game seven of the finals. You wait and see."

As a physician, I understand how it is. While I wouldn't wish Parkinson's disease on anybody, I am not ashamed to say I wish I hadn't gotten it. I am not ashamed to be as human as the next guy.

I watched a bit more of the news, and then I shut the TV off again. I'd check back later. The weather forecast was calling for more rain tomorrow. A deluge on Saturday and one slated for Sunday as well. That didn't sound good for San Antonio. A small upper-level disturbance was hovering off to the west. I began to wonder if I should've built an ark for Tweetie and me.

9

Life improved markedly after my DBS surgery in 2002. The symptoms of my Parkinson's disease became more manageable, though I obviously wasn't cured, not by a long shot. All the neurostimulator could do was zap the targeted areas inside my brain with electrical current that blocked the disruptive electrical nerve signals that were causing all the problems. My work as a geriatrician continued with less stress as well. I'd set up a small private practice the previous year, and I was striving to make a go of it. I also worked part time at a variety of local institutions and chiropractic practices that cared for the elderly.

I still found it difficult to maintain an income. I still faced discrimination more often than not. In fact, in some medical circles chiropractors are viewed as quacks unworthy of being called "doctor." I found myself working for chiropractors. They were among the few professionals that were willing to give me a chance. Prisons also were accepting of me. It took a lot of willpower to put my ego on a lower rung of the self-worth ladder, but I did it because I had to.

One condition I had to submit to in order to practice medicine struck me as quite onerous at best. The state regulators in Texas required me to undergo monitoring to ensure I was in fact capable of treating patients. While dementia can occur in some patients with Parkinson's, it isn't a given that everyone with the disease will lose cognitive function. Indeed, dementia typically presents when the person gets old and when the disease is in a very advanced stage of development. Nevertheless, the powers-that-be insisted that I jump through hoops that made little sense to me.

Every month, I had to see a psychiatrist ostensibly to determine if I was losing my ability to think clearly and to make sure I wasn't clinically depressed. Every four months I had to take time off to endure a similar grilling from a forensic psychiatrist. I still don't get why this guy was necessary. It seemed a waste of time to me, especially since I had to drive for many hours through heavy traffic in Austin to see him. I'd cool my heels in his waiting room and try not to fume. I tried to get over the perceived indignity of having to submit to an interrogation session simply to conform to regulations that felt a lot like discrimination. The receptionist would wave me into the shrink's inner sanctum. I'd sit. He'd stare at me for a long moment, as if I were some sort of unusual specimen of human he found distasteful, repellent, and discomforting.

"Well, how are we today, Dr. C?"

"Fine."

"Really? Oh, well, uh, that's great!"

The forensic psychiatrist was a rotund little shit with a mop of curly black hair, a pallid complexion that reminded me of the cadavers I encountered in medical school, and a voice that had the same effect on me as running fingernails on a blackboard.

"I'd be even better if I didn't have to drive here every four months," I said, crossing my arms over my chest and meeting his eyes with a steady stare.

He sighed, leaned back in his chair, and made steeples of his fingers. "I am sensing hostility. Hostility isn't good, Dr. C. It really isn't."

"You sense correctly. I have been coming here for two years because the state isn't sure it can trust me. Wouldn't you be annoyed?"

"Rules are rules, Dr. C."

It was my turn to sigh. "So I'm told."

"Are you taking your meds?"

"Yes."

"How are you sleeping at night."

"Fine. Unless the hose from my damn CPAP gets loose. Then all bets are off," I said.

"No more nightmares? Insomnia?"

"No more nightmares or insomnia," I repeated.

And so it would go, and I had to pay good money for the dubious privilege of enduring the man's inane questions.

Every four months I also had to see a neurologist DBS calibrator. Seeing the neurologist made sense to me, although it was inconvenient. After all, I was now battery operated. I was robot man. The robot had to keep Mr. Parkinson's from rearing up and grabbing me by the throat again.

As time passed and I ushered 2005 in alone, I began to feel Mr. P exerting his nasty influence over me again. The battery under my right collarbone was running down. The errant signals from my brain were getting through to my muscles with increasing clarity. It was like the radar-jamming plane had stopped working properly, allowing enemy antiaircraft fire to hit the squadron. I scheduled myself for battery replacement surgery. I knew that repeated surgeries would be the price I'd have to pay if DBS was to continue working. There are always tradeoffs in life, and I figured this was one of them.

I went into surgery in early April. Dr. Gauge installed a new battery. The tremors decreased to manageable levels. Yet, a short time later, my battery alarm warned of excessively low voltage. A battery that was supposed to last for two or three years was on the verge of dying. The doctors were puzzled. I was furious.

"Something is wrong," I said. "This can't be happening!" I told one of my neurologists.

"You are right, Dr. C. This isn't normal. Something is causing the voltage drain, and right now we don't know what it is. It's possible the DBS procedure needs to be repeated. But this time with brain mapping."

"Shouldn't that have been done in the first place? Brain mapping, I mean?"

Silence. The doctor looked distinctly uncomfortable. Then he said that brain mapping would have been best, but that the process was relatively new in the United States three years earlier. Many medical centers couldn't do it. I knew that, of course, but it was cold comfort to me now that it seemed I'd failed to get a critical element of DBS surgery in the first procedure. The failure was coming back to haunt me.

"You have to understand, Dr. C. We've come a long way in a short time with DBS surgery."

Not soon enough for me, I thought.

Today, DBS is light years ahead of where it was even a decade ago, and it is considered a highly effective way to combat the symptoms of Parkinson's disease in patients that don't benefit from treatment with medications alone. The use of brain mapping is now standard operating procedure, whereas it wasn't when I first entered the brave new world of DBS. Simply put, brain mapping is a bit like an electrocardiogram recording, only for your brain, not your heart. It allows the neurosurgeon to more precisely identify the specific area of the brain, or target that sends out the signals that cause the tremors in Parkinson's patients. Once the doctor has the target area lined up, he or she can properly position the electrodes. Dr. Gauge made his best guest the first time without the use of advanced technology. It proved to be a big mistake.

I was back in the OR in early August, ready for the ordeal to come. When it was all over, the precise targets were identified through a CT scan and brain mapping, and the electrodes were properly positioned to deliver maximum relief with the minimal amount of voltage. It was also discovered that the left electrode, or lead, was damaged, accounting for much of the excessive voltage drain. The lead may have broken during a recent fall I'd suffered. That was the most logical explanation. The danger of a fall breaking a DBS lead had never occurred to me. After that third surgery, I watched where

I'm going more vigilantly than I ever did before, and I still do. Falls are a leading cause of elderly people ending up in nursing homes. Balance can be impaired when you suffer from Parkinson's disease, making falls a threat that should be taken very seriously.

Now that I no longer had to put my heart and soul into fighting the dead batteries and my ongoing war with Mr. Parkinson's, I could concentrate on more positive things, like salvaging a career that had floundered since my diagnosis. I could also concentrate on building some sort of social life. I was desperately lonely. When I came home from work at night, I fed the cat and ate a simple dinner while listening to classical music. My reiki candles filled the living room with a wonderful soothing fragrance.

At times, I checked out Internet dating sites. The thought of dating again scared me, but by the same token the thought of spending the rest of my life alone didn't appeal to me much either. Human beings aren't wired for solitary existences. Even hermits generally have animals as companions. I wondered sometimes if I had turned into a hermit, a sort of urban mountain man prowling the peaks of steel skyscrapers and living off crumbs in the midst of vital and vibrant San Antonio. Unlike the mountain men, I didn't choose to run away from civilization and humanity. In some ways, it ran away from me. Still, I was in a better place now, an up time, as it were, and that's when I met Pam.

Pam had placed an ad in the personals posted on the Internet. I read her profile, looked at her picture, thought more and more about her. She was gorgeous. Naturally, she was blonde, just like Wendy and Monique. I have a certain type of lady that gets me going in the sexual department. I fall for the same sort of body type every time, and Pam was no exception. When we finally went on our first date, my reaction to Pam was profound. We made passionate love that same evening. For me, the sexual release was seismic. I felt like a man again instead of a reclusive monk. I felt hope for the first time in many years. I entertained the notion that I might be happy living with Pam for the rest of my life.

I lurched awake from a deep sleep yet again, dozing in and out since I'd gone to bed the previous evening. I checked the clock on the nightstand beside my bed. It was mid-afternoon, and the rain continued to fall. I lay on top of the unmade sheets and listened to the spatter of drops hit the windows and drum incessantly on the roof. It seemed to me that the parade of thunderstorms was lessening in intensity that the weather system that had caused so much pain and havoc upon San Antonio was moving off like an angry bear in the woods after it mauled a hiker. I removed the mask of my CPAP and shut the machine off. I stretched, feeling the aches any man in his early sixties was bound to feel after a terrible night.

I went to the bathroom and splashed cold water on my face to wake myself up. I studied my reflection in the mirror. Dark half-moons accentuated the puffy swelling under my eyes, a result of fatigue and the effects of wearing a mask to combat my sleep apnea. I knew the man who stared back at me. I knew myself. God knows, I'd had six decades to pursue dreams and hopes, confront tragedy and emotional duress, and to live life as best as I could.

Yet, sometimes I look at myself and wonder who I really am. I wonder if I've become a product of Mr. P, as if Parkinson's has come into my life and taken over. In a way, I guess the disease has done just that. In a way, I may have let it, in spite of my desire to beat it into submission.

I pushed those thoughts away and walked to the window. The dark clouds were more gray than black, indicating that they were thinning and allowing the sun to shine through them. The thunder seemed farther away. I took some comfort in that. Every storm passes. It has been so since the dawn of time.

10

I remained at the window and stared out at the flooded parking lot. The storm drains in my old subdivision had not been able to cope with the torrential rain, but, then again, nowhere in San Antonio fared all that well. In my mind's eye, I ran the film of my life, watching the raindrops make squiggling patterns on the windowpane while I recalled my more recent years. The storm had forced me to sit still, to stay in place for my own safety. It had summoned demons and angels. It had stirred memories I did not necessarily want to go over again. Yet, the life of a person really is a little like a movie. The past can be replayed over and over again, sometimes to our own detriment.

Much had changed since my divorce from Pam two years earlier, a messy vituperative affair that still caused emotional anguish on many levels. I thought back to when our son was just a baby instead of the young boy he is now. His plaintive cries brought us up short, interrupting a terrible fight. Pam and I stood looking at each other, the anger crackling between us like lightning. If the conflict wasn't about the lack of money, it was about her mistakenly thinking I was having affairs with nurses at work.

"Do you want to get him?" I asked.

She said nothing. She hugged herself tight across her chest.

"Okay," I said, turning my back on her. "I'll get him."

"You do that. You don't know what I go through. You don't understand at all."

I ignored Pam and went into the nursery. I picked my beautiful baby up, cradling him in my arms. He'd been born on my birthday, on June 21, except he came into the world in 2006 and I had arrived in 1952. As I rocked him gently in my arms, cooing and comforting him as best as I could, a terrible weight pressed on me. It seemed that I'd made a mistake with Pam, just as I had with Wendy and Monique. I'd begun to suspect she was bipolar not long after we began our torrid love affair and plunged headlong together into a marriage that should never have been. We fed off each other's negativity. We poked and prodded. Every time we fought, the voltage drain on my battery skyrocketed, forcing robot man to go into surgery three times between 2007 and 2010.

As I stood at the window, I relived the trauma of those surgeries. How I awoke with my head and neck temporarily paralyzed and a crown knocked out during intubation. It turned out that the battery was defective, which was causing the paralysis. I begged for a rechargeable lithium ion battery, but I was denied the new technology. The "experts" said I had a "high fidget factor" as a busy physician. In plain English, they didn't think I'd have time to charge the battery for the required one to two hours each day. These batteries have a charger you plug into a wall socket, and then you plug the charger into your battery to bring the voltage back up to acceptable levels. It's a bit like being an electric car. The battery can last up to ten years, and someday I hope to get one. After the divorce, I went through another robot man routine surgery in August 2012. I'm due for another battery replacement soon. At this point, I don't have any other choice.

I've paid a heavy price for the relief I receive from DBS. In the last three years, the current from the electrodes has seriously degraded my speech. When I talk, it can be hard for people to understand what I'm trying to say. Rapid speech is impossible. Long conversations are tough. It's as if a curtain of complete isolation has enveloped me in a dark embrace, and while I fight it I often think Mr. Parkinson's is coming out the winner. Extensive speech therapy will help, or so I'm told. I have that to look forward to, and perhaps I'll see improvement one day.

The demise of my marriage hit me hard, but I cherish the gift of my son. I treasure him more than anything else in this world, though I don't get to see him much because of the antipathy between Pam and me. When he was born, I had some of his umbilical chord cryogenically frozen to preserve the stem cells in case either of us needs them. I pray for advances in embryonic-stem-cell research that could someday make it possible to grow colonies of dopamine-producing cells to replace the ones that die due to Parkinson's disease. In recent years, I have been convinced that the studies involving stem-cell research show great promise in coming up with a cure for the disease.

Maybe it's not too late for me, I thought as I turned on the TV. San Antonio's mayor and fire chief were holding a press conference.

More than ten inches of rain had fallen on the city since midnight, most of it within a four-hour period. The news footage reminded me of the great Mississippi flood of 1993. On Sunday morning, the San Antonio River near Elmendorf was expected to peak at sixty-two feet, or nearly twice the height of normal flood stage at thirty-five feet.

A public warning appeared on the crawl at the bottom of the screen. "This is a life-threatening situation. If you are in the area of the San Antonio and have been flooded before, you will be flooded again." Evacuations were under way. Rescue efforts were ongoing.

I got up and turned off the TV. The chaos of life was in evidence throughout San Antonio. I needed no more of it in my life for the moment. I scooped Tweetie up in my arms and pet her. She began to purr. In the distance, a clap of thunder sounded muffled and weak. I would pick myself up again after the rejection from the clinic and keep on keeping on, just like the good people of San Antonio would recover and move forward after the storm waters receded.

"Yes," I whispered, "without hope there is nothing."

Flower Day, 1925: consciously hieratic, bowed under an angelic load

Levels of graphic sophistication lying beneath the populist surface.